HAL LEONARD
BANJO SCALE FINDER

by CHAD JOHNSON

ISBN 978-0-634-06439-5

HAL•LEONARD®
CORPORATION
7777 W. BLUEMOUND RD. P.O. BOX 13819 MILWAUKEE, WI 53213

In Australia Contact:
Hal Leonard Australia Pty. Ltd
22 Taunton Drive P.O. Box 5130
Cheltenham East, 3192 Victoria, Australia
Email: ausadmin@halleonard.com

Visit Hal Leonard Online at
www.halleonard.com

CONTENTS

INTRODUCTION

The purpose of *Banjo Scale Finder* is to present diagrams for the most often-used scales and modes in an orderly and easily accessible fashion. You can use it simply as a reference guide when you want to quickly get a scale under your fingers or as the foundation for creating an in-depth practice routine. Its logical organization and comprehensive approach will provide you with the tools you need to gain a serious command of the banjo fretboard, while at the same time familiarizing you with the sounds of the scales used in almost all Western music.

Why are scales so important?

Scales are the building blocks of music. An understanding of scale construction is the first step in grasping the bigger concepts of chord theory and improvisation, to name but a few. Music is not only an art; it's a language as well. Just as it benefits us to learn how words are spelled and constructed, it benefits us to know how scales are spelled and constructed. It allows us to communicate better with other musicians and flesh out our musical ideas more quickly.

Although some musicians claim that learning scales and theory detracts from their creativity and inspiration, there is absolutely no basis for this assumption. Does a writer's well dry up after learning the basic rules of grammar? Of course not! (He obviously learned the basic rules of grammar before he began to write.)

Perhaps the most important reason to learn scales though is the freedom it grants you. If you want to spend the rest of your banjo playing days plunking out open-position chords, then perhaps you don't need this book. If, however, you'd like to be creative in your banjo playing and play more than chords or root notes, the learning of scales will greatly expedite the process. It will help you avoid spending your precious rehearsal time fumbling around the fretboard, searching for that elusive note or line you hear in your head. And let's face it—no one likes to sit around waiting for another band member to get his act together!

HOW TO USE THIS BOOK

Banjo Scale Finder makes learning scales both fast and easy. Over 1,300 commonly used scale patterns are literally at your fingertips!

The Scale Diagrams

Each scale is first presented in a "whole neck" diagram, which shows the entire banjo fretboard through the twelfth fret. Following are several different scale "patterns." Pattern 1 will always begin with the root note of the scale on the fourth string. The remaining patterns then progress through the scale, each one beginning on the next note. In other words, pattern 2 will begin on the second note of the scale, pattern 3 will begin on the third note of the scale, etc. Since most scales include seven different notes, there will usually be seven different patterns. The patterns continue up the neck until they exceed the twelfth fret, at which point they are transposed down an octave. For scales that contain less than seven different notes—like the pentatonic and blues scales for instance—"alternate" scale patterns are included in the place of the sixth and/or seventh pattern. If you're unfamiliar with how scale diagrams are read, here's a detailed explanation:

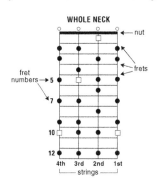
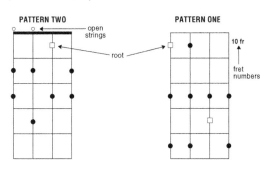

Playing Through the Scale Patterns

When possible, use the one-finger-per-fret rule for fingering these scale shapes. That is to say, use your first finger for the first fret in the shape, the second finger for the second fret, etc. For the instances where more than four frets are covered, you'll need to either stretch your hand or shift positions to accommodate.

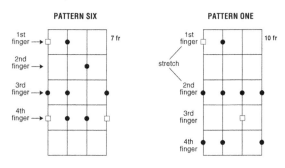

A diagram of the entire banjo neck is provided here for reference:

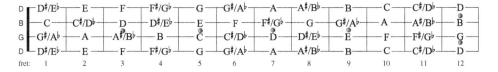

A BRIEF DISCUSSION ON SCALE CONSTRUCTION

The Circle of Fifths

Although it's beyond the scope of this book to cover all the aspects of music theory, there are a few things you'll need to know before proceeding. The first of those is the *Circle of Fifths*. This is a diagram that helps in understanding the relationship of different keys in music. When something is said to be "in the key of D," this means that D is the *tonic* chord—the chord that feels like home or feels resolved. Many times, this will be the last chord of a phrase or the last chord of an entire song. Each different key possesses its own *key signature*. The key signature is the collection of sharps or flats you see at the beginning of a musical piece. This tells the performer that those notes are to be played as sharps or flats throughout the entire piece of music. (The key of C has no sharps or flats, so its key signature looks blank.)

Although it is not essential for you to memorize the circle right now, it's provided here as a reference for when learning the material throughout the book. Memorization is certainly encouraged though, as it will greatly aid in your musical development. It may seem like a lot to learn at once, but there are patterns at work that make the process fairly simple.

Notice that, when moving to the right (the "sharps" side), each new key contains the same sharps as the previous and adds one more. Moving to the left (the "flats" side) works the same way. Keep this in mind when learning each new key signature. The parentheses indicate each major key's *relative minor* key. Relative major and minor keys contain the same key signature; they just start and end the scale on two different notes. This will be explained more in depth in the "Improvising and Soloing" section.

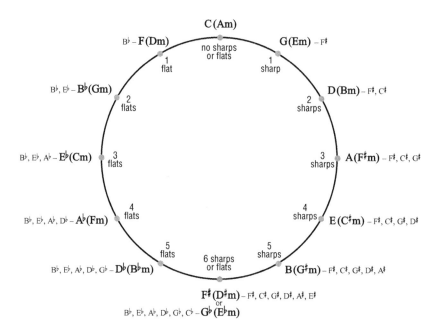

Intervals

If you're just starting from scratch and have no experience with scales at all, let's talk briefly about the basics before jumping in. A *scale* is simply a collection of notes arranged in a certain order. There are many different types of scales, and each one possesses a slightly different *intervallic formula*. An *interval* is simply another name for the distance between two notes. In terms of scales, intervals are usually measured in half steps (one fret on the banjo) and whole steps (two frets on the banjo). Let's start with the major scale.

The intervallic formula for any major scale is always: whole step–whole step–half step–whole step–whole step–whole step–half step. This is demonstrated in the C major scale below:

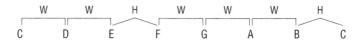

The C major scale is the only major scale that contains no accidentals (sharps or flats). This is most easily confirmed on a piano keyboard, as it contains only white notes.

Numeric Formula

Scales also contain a *numeric formula*. The major scale, for example, contains seven different notes, beginning again an octave higher on what would be the eighth note. These notes are numbered as scale degrees: 1–7. The major scale is the standard by which we define all other scales when using this number method. In other words, a major scale will consist of 1–2–3–4–5–6–7. Other scales will have one or more of these numbers altered (flatted or sharped). For instance, the minor scale's numeric formula looks like this: 1–2–♭3–4–5–♭6–♭7. So, for instance, a C minor scale would possess the same notes as a C major scale, but the 3rd, 6th, and 7th notes would be lowered by a half step (flatted). See the example below:

C major scale

C minor scale

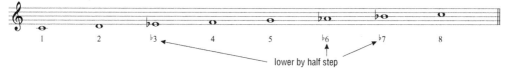

lower by half step

THE SCALES AND MODES

Before we get into learning the scale patterns on the banjo, let's briefly touch upon each scale covered in this book. Each scale here will be presented with C as its root note.

Major Scale (Ionian Mode)
Formula: 1–2–3–4–5–6–7

The major scale is by far the most important scale you'll ever learn. It forms the harmonic basis for almost all Western music. By beginning and ending on the different notes of this scale (for instance playing the scale from the 2nd degree up to the octave 2nd degree), we get the seven different *modes*. The first mode, Ionian, is simply another name for the major scale.

Dorian Mode
Formula: 1–2–♭3–4–5–6–♭7

Dorian is the second mode of the major scale and, along with the Mixolydian, is the most widely used after the Ionian and Aeolian modes, commonly found in rock, blues, latin, and jazz styles. It's very similar to the minor scale (only one note is different) but contains a slightly brighter sound.

Phrygian Mode
Formula: 1–♭2–♭3–4–5–♭6–♭7

The third mode of the major scale is Phrygian, another mode which differs from the Aeolian by only one note. This mode possesses an exotic sound that is commonly heard in flamenco music. The flatted 2nd degree is largely responsible for the unique flavor of this mode.

Lydian Mode
Formula: 1–2–3–♯4–5–6–7

The Lydian mode can be described as a major scale with a raised 4th degree; all of the other notes are the same. The sound of this scale is very bright and is commonly used in jazz and especially films. This is the scale you often hear at the end of a movie preview when "coming in September" appears on the screen.

Mixolydian Mode
Formula: 1–2–3–4–5–6–♭7

The Mixolydian mode can be described as a major scale with a flatted 7th degree. This scale possesses a similar sound to a major scale but with a bluesy edge. It's used often in jazz, blues, and rock 'n' roll. Along with Dorian, it's next in popularity behind the Ionian and Aeolian modes.

Natural Minor Scale (Aeolian Mode)
Formula: 1–2–♭3–4–5–♭6–♭7

The minor scale, or Aeolian mode, possesses a dark, sad sound as opposed to the bright, happy sound of major. This is the sixth mode of the major scale and is used almost as frequently as the major scale in most all forms of Western music.

Locrian Mode
Formula: 1–♭2–♭3–4–♭5–♭6–♭7

The seventh and final mode of the major scale is the Locrian mode. Because of the flatted 5th degree in this scale, the tonic chord is actually a diminished chord. (All of the other modes feature either major or minor chords as their tonic.) This makes this mode sound very unstable, and it doesn't see much action aside from some jazz, fusion, or certain types of heavy metal.

Major Pentatonic

Formula: 1–2–3–5–6

You may have noticed that only five numbers are listed in this scale's numeric formula. That's because the term "pentatonic" refers to five-note scales. In this case, the major pentatonic is simply a major scale with no 4th or 7th degrees. Many improvisations are based upon pentatonic scales, as they contain relatively all "safe" notes.

Minor Pentatonic

Formula: 1–♭3–4–5–♭7

The minor pentatonic simply deletes the 2nd and ♭6th degrees from the minor scale. This is an extremely popular scale, used not only in improvising but also in creating riffs.

Blues Scale

Formula: 1–♭3–4–♭5–5–♭7

The blues scale adds a note to the minor pentatonic to create a six-note scale with two consecutive half steps. As suggested by the name, the scale contains a bluesy quality and is often used interchangeably with the minor pentatonic in improvisations.

Harmonic Minor Scale

Formula: 1–2–♭3–4–5–♭6–7

Aside from the seven modes and pentatonic scales, there are still plenty of other usable scales. The harmonic minor scale can be thought of as a natural minor scale with a raised 7th degree. The exotic tonality of this scale comes from the interval between the ♭6th and the 7th tone of 1 ½ steps. This scale was used largely in classical music of the Baroque and classical era (even more so than the natural minor scale). It arose from the desire to have a leading-tone relationship (a half step between the 7th and tonic) in a minor scale, providing a more definite resolution.

Melodic Minor Scale

Formula: 1–2–♭3–4–5–6–7

The melodic minor scale was created after the harmonic minor scale. Finding the unusual interval between the ♭6th and 7th degrees of the Harmonic minor scale awkward and difficult to sing when ascending, composers began raising the 6th degrees in a minor scale as well. However, the natural minor scale was then often used when descending. This distinguishes the melodic minor as the only scale that's spelled differently when ascending than when descending. In modern practice, however, the ascending form (the formula given) is often used exclusively as a scale all its own, mostly in jazz and fusion.

Mixo-Blues Scale

Formula: 1–2–♭3–3–4–♭5–5–6–♭7

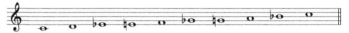

The Mixo-blues scale is actually the combined notes from a Mixolydian mode (1–2–3–4–5–6–♭7) and the blues scale (1–♭3–4 –♭5–5–♭7). This scale is used extensively when improvising over bluesy progressions in major keys. It's important to remember, however, that just because both the ♭3rd and ♮3rd are included in this scale, they don't have to be played in tandem all the time. Often times, a player may play one lick from the blues scale, another lick from the Mixolydian mode, and then one lick that combines them. This approach is what is referred to as the Mixo-blues scale.

Half-Whole Diminished Scale

Formula: 1–♭2–♭3–3–♯4–5–6–♭7

There are two types of diminished scales, and each one contains eight different notes. Each one consists of alternating whole and half steps, and the only difference between the two lies in the order of these. The half-whole diminished scale begins with a half step first and then proceeds with alternating whole and half steps. This particular scale is very frequently used in jazz music over altered dominant chords.

An interesting thing to note about diminished scales is that they are *symmetrical* scales. Since they feature a repeated pattern, every other note in the scale could basically be considered the root of the scale. In other words, a C diminished scale will contain the same notes as the E♭, F♯, and A diminished scales. So there are really only three different half-whole diminished scales:

C dim   = E♭ dim, F♯ dim, and A dim

C♯ dim = E dim, G dim, and B♭ dim

D dim   = F dim, A♭ dim, and B dim

Whole-Half Diminished Scale

Formula: 1–2–♭3–4–♭5–♭6–6–7

The lesser common of the diminished scales is the whole-half type. This is the opposite of the half-whole scale; it begins with a whole step first and then proceeds with alternating half and whole steps. It's commonly used over fully diminished or half diminished chords. The whole-half scale is symmetrical as well, meaning there are only three different ones, just as we saw above with the half-whole diminished scale.

Whole Tone Scale

Formula: 1–2–3–♯4–♯5–♯6

Consisting of nothing but whole steps, the whole tone scale is another symmetrical scale. Whereas there are only three different diminished scales, there are actually only two different whole-tone scales! A C whole-tone scale will have the same notes as D, E, F♯, G♯, and A♯, while a C♯ whole-tone will have the same notes as D♯, F, G, A, and B. The scale was commonly used by composers in the nineteenth century, namely Claude Debussy. Jazz and fusion players often make use of the scale's unique tonality as well when improvising and composing.

Chromatic Scale

Formula: 1–♭2–2–♭3–3–4–♭5–5–♭6–6–♭7–7

The chromatic scale contains all twelve notes in the musical alphabet, and therefore it doesn't really have a "root"; every note could be the root. While the scale is commonly employed in fingering exercises, it's important to note that the scale is rarely played in its entirety during actual musical applications. It's much more likely that fragments of the scale would be used to color certain phrases here and there.

IMPROVISING AND SOLOING

It won't really do you much good to learn all these new scales if you don't have any idea how to apply them. In this section, we'll take a look at two different approaches you can use in determining what scales to use and when. Since the main focus of this book is to show you how to play the scales, we don't have the space to adequately cover all the bases on this subject. However, this should at least get you pointed in the right direction. There are many books available dedicated to the subject of scale usage that you can use to further your abilities once you have these scales under your fingers.

Using One Scale Over the Entire Progression

Perhaps the easiest and most commonly used approach to soloing is the major- or minor-scale approach for the whole progression. In this approach, after determining which key the song is in, you simply apply the appropriate major or minor scale and use it throughout the song. You can usually determine the key of a song from the key signature. For instance, if the key signature is two sharps and D seems to be the tonic chord, the song is most likely in the key of D major. If the progression seems to center around B minor, however, then we would call that the tonic chord, and the progression would be in the key of B minor, the *relative* minor of D major. As we learned earlier, major keys and their relative minors share the same key signature. Each major key's relative minor can be found by locating the 6th degree of the scale. We can confirm that B minor is relative to D major by counting through the notes of the D major scale: D (1), E (2), F# (3), G (4), A (5), and B (6). So, the keys of D major and B minor make use of the same chords, but the stress will be placed differently depending on whether the song is major or minor.

In terms of what scales to use, it's pretty much a no-brainer. If the song were in D major, for example, you could use the D major scale or D major pentatonic throughout. If it were in D minor (the relative of F major), you could use the D minor scale or D minor pentatonic throughout. How did we know that D minor is the relative of F major? Well, the Circle of Fifths tells us, for one. We can also count through the notes of the F major scale to confirm that D is the 6th degree.

What if, however, you don't have a piece of music in front of you? Maybe all you have is some chords, or perhaps you're figuring out some chords by ear off the stereo. If you're having trouble determining the key, try using the chart below. Simply find the line that contains all the chords of the song you're working on, and you've got the key. If the chords fit into more than one line, determine which chord the progression centers around—which chord feels resolved when you play it—and that's most likely the key.

There will be songs that change keys or contain certain *non-diatonic* chords (chords that are not in the key). For these songs, you'll need to experiment with other scales during those moments. Many songs, however, will fit neatly into one key, and you'll be able to use the same scale throughout the entire song. By listening closely to how each note of the scale reacts to the different chords, you'll train your ear in determining which notes to stress and when.

major keys ———   ——— minor keys ———

I Ionian	ii Dorian	iii Phrygian	IV Lydian	V Mixolydian	vi Aeolian	vii° Locrian
C	Dm	Em	F	G	Am	B°
D♭	E♭m	Fm	G♭	A♭	B♭m	C°
D	Em	F#m	G	A	Bm	C#°
E♭	Fm	Gm	A♭	B♭	Cm	D°
E	F#m	G#m	A	B	C#m	D#°
F	Gm	Am	B♭	C	Dm	E°
F#	G#m	A#m	B	C#	D#m	E#°
G	Am	Bm	C	D	Em	F#°
A♭	B♭m	Cm	D♭	E♭	Fm	G°
A	Bm	C#m	D	E	F#m	G#°
B♭	Cm	Dm	E♭	F	Gm	A°
B	C#m	D#m	E	F#	G#m	A#°

If, when determining a song's key with the chart above, you couldn't quite pinpoint it, the song may be in a mode. For example, if the song's chords were G, F, Em, and C, but the progression seemed to revolve around G instead of C, try looking at the top where the modes are listed. In this case, the song is in G Mixolydian, and you can use the G Mixolydian mode when playing over it. If a song contained the chords Dm, F, G, and C, but Dm seemed to be the tonic chord, we could deduce by looking along the top that the song is in D Dorian, and that mode should be used.

Chord-by-Chord Approach

Occasionally, a song will have several chords that don't seem to be related at all. In these instances, you might have to use a different scale or mode for each chord. For example, let's say a song's chord progression goes like this: C–E♭–C♯m–F. These four chords won't fit into any of the lines in the chart above, so they are obviously not from the same key. (Playing through them once will make that obvious as well.) In this instance, you'll need to apply a different scale to each chord. Since the C, E♭, and F chords are major, you can choose between any one of the major scales or modes listed below for each. The C♯m chord will require one of the minor scales or modes to sound best. Since there are no diminished chords in the progression, the Locrian mode or diminished scales will not be used.

So, for this particular progression, your scale choice could be something like: C Lydian, E♭ Ionian, C♯ Dorian, and F major pentatonic. Or maybe you'd choose C Mixolydian, E♭ Lydian, C♯ Melodic minor, and the F major scale (F Ionian). In chord progressions such as these, use your ear to determine which sounds best to you. There are no "right" or "wrong" answers in this case. If it sounds good to you, then it is good. Experiment with all the chords and scales below and have fun!

Chord type	Formula	Scale	Mode
Major	1-3-5	Major, major pentatonic	Ionian, Lydian, Mixolydian
Minor	1-♭3-5	Minor, minor pentatonic, blues	Dorian, Phrygian, Aeolian
Diminished	1-♭3-♭5	Diminished	Locrian
Augmented	1-3-♯5	Whole tone	
Major 7th	1-3-5-7	Major, major pentatonic	Ionian, Lydian
Minor 7th	1-♭3-5-♭7	Minor, minor pentatonic	Dorian, Phrygian, Aeolian
Dominant 7th	1-3-5-♭7	*Blues, Mixo-blues	Mixolydian

* Though the blues scale is technically a minor-based scale, it's commonly used over dominant seventh chords in bluesy styles.

C MAJOR (IONIAN)

WHOLE NECK | PATTERN ONE | PATTERN TWO | PATTERN THREE

C DORIAN

WHOLE NECK | PATTERN ONE | PATTERN TWO | PATTERN THREE

C PHRYGIAN

WHOLE NECK | PATTERN ONE | PATTERN TWO | PATTERN THREE

C LYDIAN

WHOLE NECK | PATTERN ONE | PATTERN TWO | PATTERN THREE

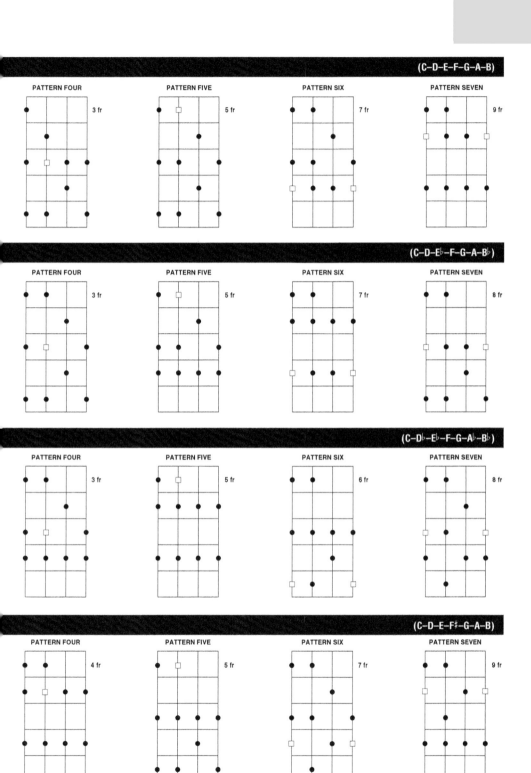

17

C MIXOLYDIAN

WHOLE NECK	PATTERN ONE	PATTERN TWO	PATTERN THREE

C MINOR (AEOLIAN)

WHOLE NECK	PATTERN ONE	PATTERN TWO	PATTERN THREE

C LOCRIAN

WHOLE NECK	PATTERN ONE	PATTERN TWO	PATTERN THREE

C MAJOR PENTATONIC

WHOLE NECK	PATTERN ONE	PATTERN TWO	PATTERN THREE

PATTERN FOUR — 3 fr

PATTERN FIVE — 5 fr

PATTERN SIX — 7 fr

PATTERN SEVEN — 8 fr

PATTERN FOUR — 3 fr

PATTERN FIVE — 5 fr

PATTERN SIX — 6 fr

PATTERN SEVEN — 8 fr

PATTERN FOUR — 3 fr

PATTERN FIVE — 4 fr

PATTERN SIX — 6 fr

PATTERN SEVEN — 8 fr

PATTERN FOUR — 5 fr

PATTERN FIVE — 7 fr

ALT. PATTERN ONE — 9 fr

ALT. PATTERN TWO — 10 fr

19

C MINOR PENTATONIC

WHOLE NECK	PATTERN ONE	PATTERN TWO	PATTERN THREE
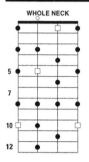	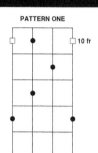	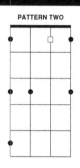	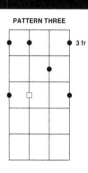

C BLUES

WHOLE NECK	PATTERN ONE	PATTERN TWO	PATTERN THREE
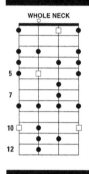	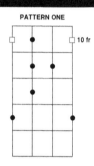		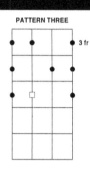

C HARMONIC MINOR

WHOLE NECK	PATTERN ONE	PATTERN TWO	PATTERN THREE
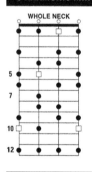	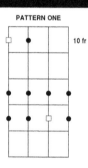	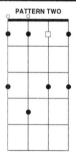	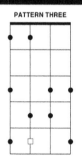

C MELODIC MINOR

WHOLE NECK	PATTERN ONE	PATTERN TWO	PATTERN THREE
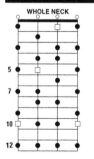	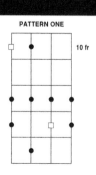	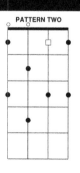	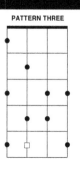

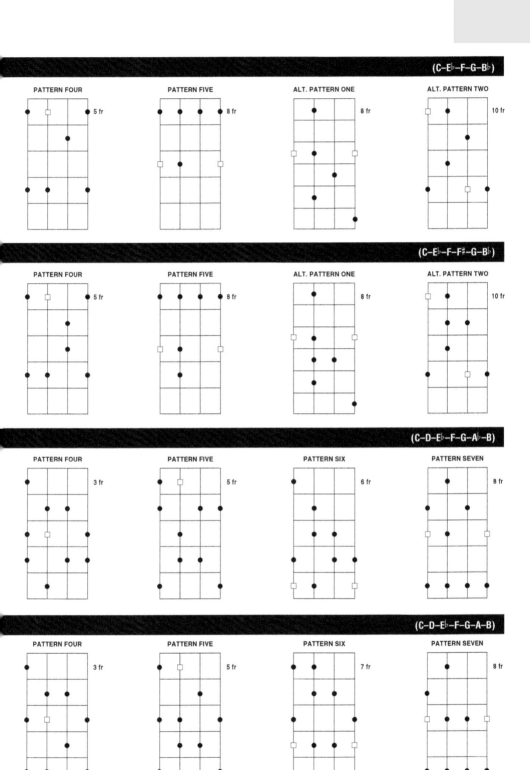

C MIXO-BLUES

WHOLE NECK | PATTERN ONE (10 fr) | PATTERN TWO | PATTERN THREE (2 fr)

C DIMINISHED (HALF-WHOLE)

WHOLE NECK | PATTERN ONE (9 fr) | PATTERN TWO (11 fr) | PATTERN THREE

C DIMINISHED (WHOLE-HALF)

WHOLE NECK | PATTERN ONE (10 fr) | PATTERN TWO (11 fr) | PATTERN THREE

C WHOLE TONE   (C–D–E–F#–Ab–Bb)

WHOLE NECK | PATTERN ONE (9 fr) | PATTERN TWO (10 fr) | PATTERN THREE (7 fr)

22

(C–D–D♯–E–F–F♯–G–A–B♭)

PATTERN FOUR
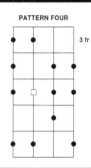
3 fr

PATTERN FIVE
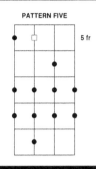
5 fr

PATTERN SIX
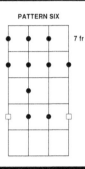
7 fr

PATTERN SEVEN
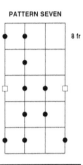
8 fr

(C–D♭–E♭–E–F♯–G–A–B♭)

PATTERN FOUR
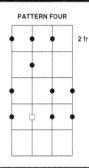
2 fr

PATTERN FIVE
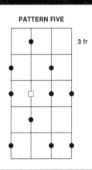
3 fr

PATTERN SIX
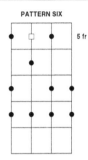
5 fr

PATTERN SEVEN
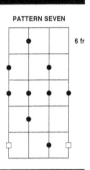
6 fr

(C–D–E♭–F–G♭–A♭–A–B)

PATTERN FOUR
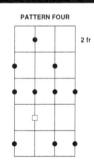
2 fr

PATTERN FIVE
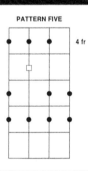
4 fr

PATTERN SIX
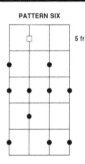
5 fr

PATTERN SEVEN
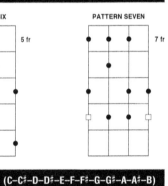
7 fr

C CHROMATIC
(C–C♯–D–D♯–E–F–F♯–G–G♯–A–A♯–B)

WHOLE NECK
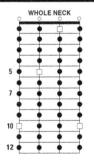

PATTERN ONE
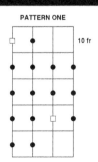
10 fr

PATTERN TWO
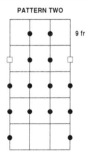
9 fr

PATTERN THREE
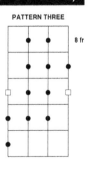
8 fr

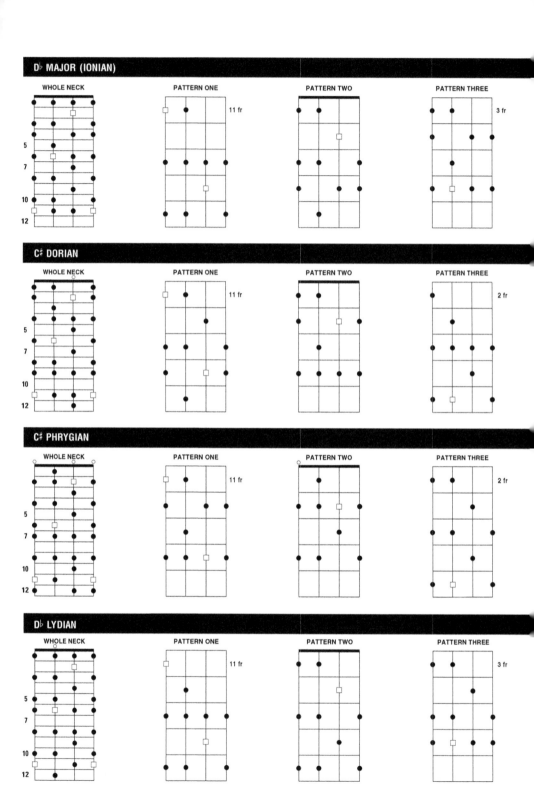

24

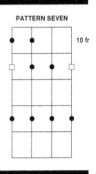

(D♭–E♭–F–G♭–A♭–B♭–C)

PATTERN FOUR	PATTERN FIVE	PATTERN SIX	PATTERN SEVEN
4 fr	6 fr	8 fr	10 fr

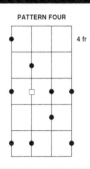
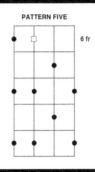
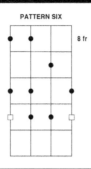
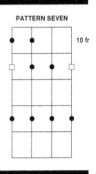

(C#–D#–E–F#–G#–A#–B)

PATTERN FOUR	PATTERN FIVE	PATTERN SIX	PATTERN SEVEN
4 fr	6 fr	8 fr	9 fr

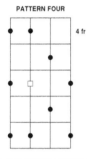
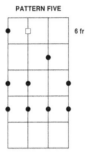
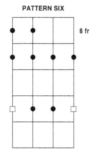
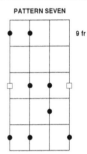

(C#–D–E–F#–G#–A–B)

PATTERN FOUR	PATTERN FIVE	PATTERN SIX	PATTERN SEVEN
4 fr	6 fr	7 fr	9 fr

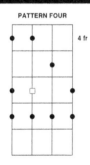
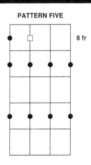
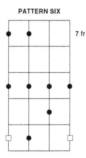
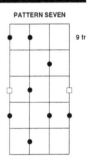

(D♭–E♭–F–G–A♭–B♭–C)

PATTERN FOUR	PATTERN FIVE	PATTERN SIX	PATTERN SEVEN
5 fr	6 fr	8 fr	10 fr

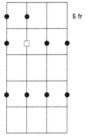
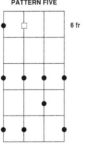
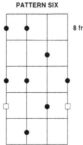
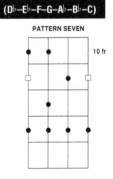

C# MIXOLYDIAN

WHOLE NECK | PATTERN ONE | PATTERN TWO | PATTERN THREE
11 fr | | 3 fr

C# MINOR (AEOLIAN)

WHOLE NECK | PATTERN ONE | PATTERN TWO | PATTERN THREE
11 fr | | 2 fr

C# LOCRIAN

WHOLE NECK | PATTERN ONE | PATTERN TWO | PATTERN THREE
11 fr | | 2 fr

Db MAJOR PENTATONIC

WHOLE NECK | PATTERN ONE | PATTERN TWO | PATTERN THREE
11 fr | | 3 fr

26

(C#–D#–E#–F#–G#–A#–B)

PATTERN FOUR	PATTERN FIVE	PATTERN SIX	PATTERN SEVEN
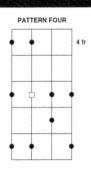 4 fr	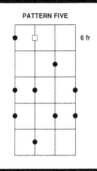 6 fr	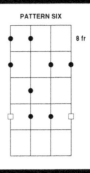 8 fr	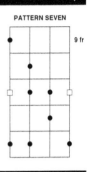 9 fr

(C#–D#–E–F#–G#–A–B)

PATTERN FOUR	PATTERN FIVE	PATTERN SIX	PATTERN SEVEN
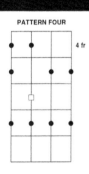 4 fr	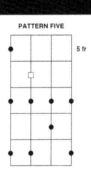 6 fr	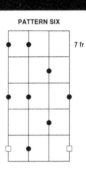 7 fr	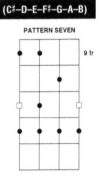 9 fr

(C#–D–E–F#–G–A–B)

PATTERN FOUR	PATTERN FIVE	PATTERN SIX	PATTERN SEVEN
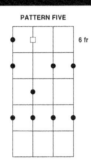 4 fr	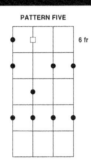 5 fr	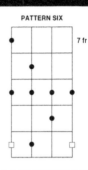 7 fr	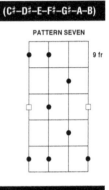 9 fr

(Db–Eb–F–Ab–Bb)

PATTERN FOUR	PATTERN FIVE	ALT. PATTERN ONE	ALT. PATTERN TWO
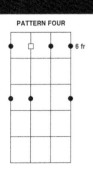 6 fr	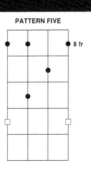 8 fr	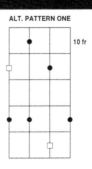 10 fr	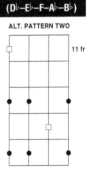 11 fr

27

C# MINOR PENTATONIC

WHOLE NECK	PATTERN ONE	PATTERN TWO	PATTERN THREE

C# BLUES

WHOLE NECK	PATTERN ONE	PATTERN TWO	PATTERN THREE

C# HARMONIC MINOR

WHOLE NECK	PATTERN ONE	PATTERN TWO	PATTERN THREE

C# MELODIC MINOR

WHOLE NECK	PATTERN ONE	PATTERN TWO	PATTERN THREE

(C#–E–F#–G#–B)

PATTERN FOUR	PATTERN FIVE	ALT. PATTERN ONE	ALT. PATTERN TWO
6 fr	9 fr	9 fr	11 fr

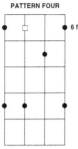 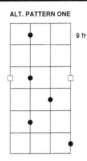 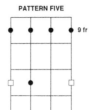 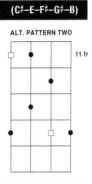

(C#–E–F#–G–G#–B)

PATTERN FOUR	PATTERN FIVE	ALT. PATTERN ONE	ALT. PATTERN TWO
6 fr	9 fr	9 fr	11 fr

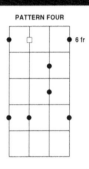 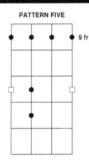 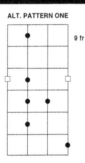 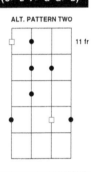

(C#–D#–E–F#–G#–A–B#)

PATTERN FOUR	PATTERN FIVE	PATTERN SIX	PATTERN SEVEN
4 fr	6 fr	7 fr	9 fr

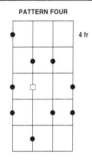 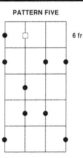 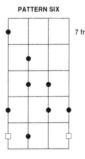 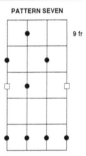

(C#–D#–E–F#–G#–A#–B#)

PATTERN FOUR	PATTERN FIVE	PATTERN SIX	PATTERN SEVEN
4 fr	6 fr	8 fr	9 fr

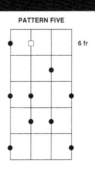 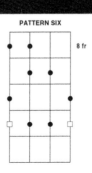 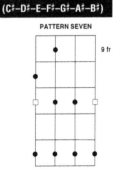

C♯ MIXO-BLUES

WHOLE NECK	PATTERN ONE	PATTERN TWO	PATTERN THREE

11 fr

3 fr

C♯ DIMINISHED (HALF-WHOLE)

WHOLE NECK	PATTERN ONE	PATTERN TWO	PATTERN THREE

10 fr

C♯ DIMINISHED (WHOLE-HALF)

WHOLE NECK	PATTERN ONE	PATTERN TWO	PATTERN THREE

11 fr

2 fr

C♯ WHOLE TONE   (C♯–D♯–E♯–G–A–B)

WHOLE NECK	PATTERN ONE	PATTERN TWO	PATTERN THREE

10 fr

11 fr

8 fr

(C#–D#–E–E#–F#–G–G#–A#–B)

PATTERN FOUR
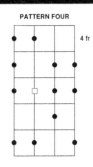
4 fr

PATTERN FIVE
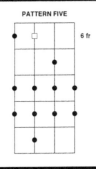
6 fr

PATTERN SIX
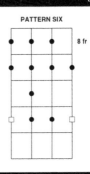
8 fr

PATTERN SEVEN
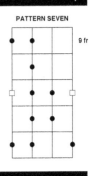
9 fr

(C#–D–E–F–G–G#–A#–B)

PATTERN FOUR
3 fr

PATTERN FIVE
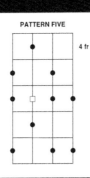
4 fr

PATTERN SIX
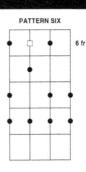
6 fr

PATTERN SEVEN
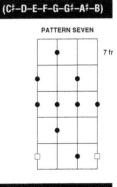
7 fr

(C#–D#–E–F#–G–A–A#–B#)

PATTERN FOUR
3 fr

PATTERN FIVE
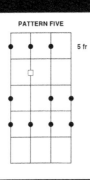
5 fr

PATTERN SIX
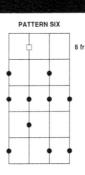
6 fr

PATTERN SEVEN
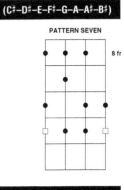
8 fr

C# CHROMATIC
(C#–D–D#–E–F–F#–G–G#–A–A#–B–B#)

WHOLE NECK
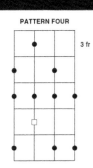
5 7 10 12

PATTERN ONE
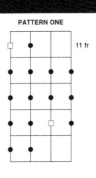
11 fr

PATTERN TWO
10 fr

PATTERN THREE
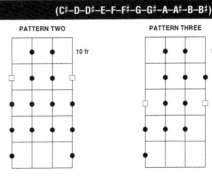
9 fr

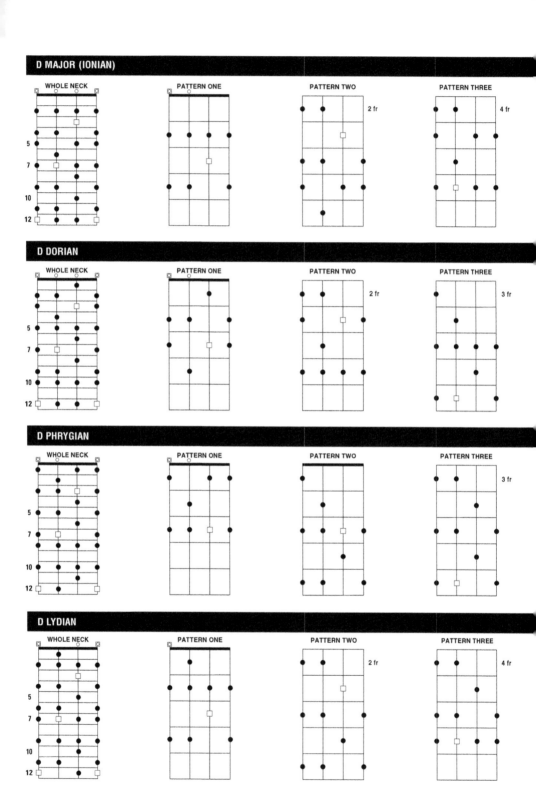

(D–E–F#–G–A–B–C#)

PATTERN FOUR
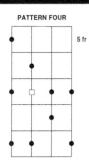
5 fr

PATTERN FIVE
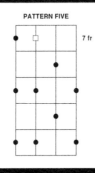
7 fr

PATTERN SIX
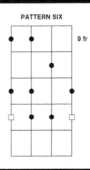
9 fr

PATTERN SEVEN
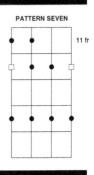
11 fr

(D–E–F–G–A–B–C)

PATTERN FOUR
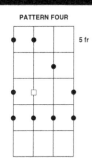
5 fr

PATTERN FIVE
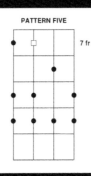
7 fr

PATTERN SIX
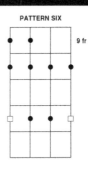
9 fr

PATTERN SEVEN
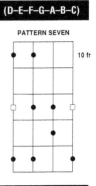
10 fr

(D–E♭–F–G–A–B♭–C)

PATTERN FOUR
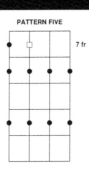
5 fr

PATTERN FIVE
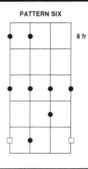
7 fr

PATTERN SIX
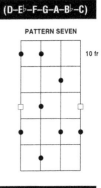
8 fr

PATTERN SEVEN
10 fr

(D–E–F#–G#–A–B–C#)

PATTERN FOUR
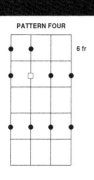
6 fr

PATTERN FIVE
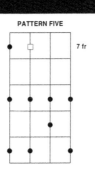
7 fr

PATTERN SIX
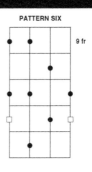
9 fr

PATTERN SEVEN
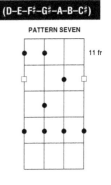
11 fr

D MIXOLYDIAN

WHOLE NECK | PATTERN ONE | PATTERN TWO | PATTERN THREE

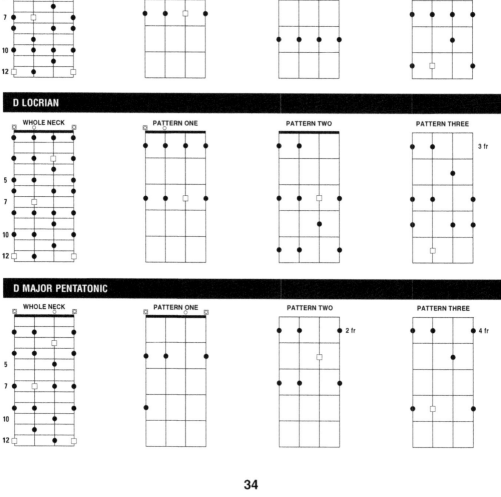

D MINOR (AEOLIAN)

WHOLE NECK | PATTERN ONE | PATTERN TWO | PATTERN THREE

D LOCRIAN

WHOLE NECK | PATTERN ONE | PATTERN TWO | PATTERN THREE

D MAJOR PENTATONIC

WHOLE NECK | PATTERN ONE | PATTERN TWO | PATTERN THREE

(D–E–F♯–G–A–B–C)

PATTERN FOUR 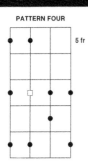 5 fr

PATTERN FIVE 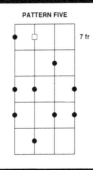 7 fr

PATTERN SIX 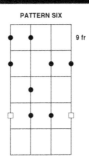 9 fr

PATTERN SEVEN 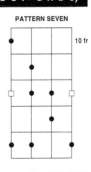 10 fr

(D–E–F–G–A–B♭–C)

PATTERN FOUR 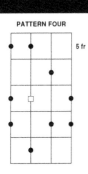 5 fr

PATTERN FIVE 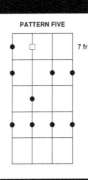 7 fr

PATTERN SIX 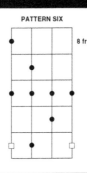 8 fr

PATTERN SEVEN 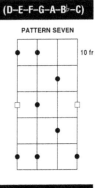 10 fr

(D–E♭–F–G–A♭–B♭–C)

PATTERN FOUR 5 fr

PATTERN FIVE 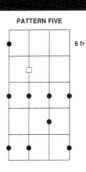 6 fr

PATTERN SIX 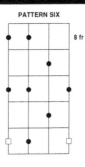 8 fr

PATTERN SEVEN 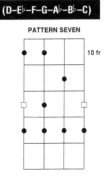 10 fr

(D–E–F♯–A–B)

PATTERN FOUR 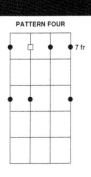 7 fr

PATTERN FIVE 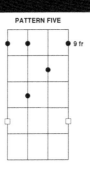 9 fr

ALT. PATTERN ONE 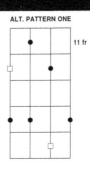 11 fr

ALT. PATTERN TWO

35

D MINOR PENTATONIC

WHOLE NECK | PATTERN ONE | PATTERN TWO | PATTERN THREE

D BLUES

WHOLE NECK | PATTERN ONE | PATTERN TWO | PATTERN THREE

D HARMONIC MINOR

WHOLE NECK | PATTERN ONE | PATTERN TWO | PATTERN THREE

D MELODIC MINOR

WHOLE NECK | PATTERN ONE | PATTERN TWO | PATTERN THREE

(D–F–G–A–C)

PATTERN FOUR
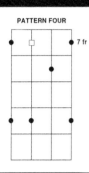
7 fr

PATTERN FIVE
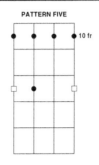
10 fr

ALT. PATTERN ONE
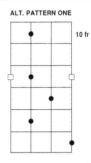
10 fr

ALT. PATTERN TWO
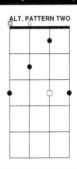

(D–F–G–G♯–A–C)

PATTERN FOUR
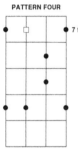
7 fr

PATTERN FIVE
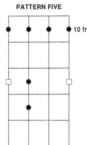
10 fr

ALT. PATTERN ONE
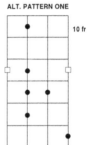
10 fr

ALT. PATTERN TWO
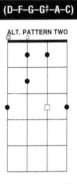

(D–E–F–G–A–B♭–C♯)

PATTERN FOUR
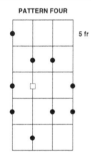
5 fr

PATTERN FIVE
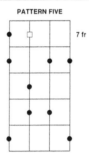
7 fr

PATTERN SIX
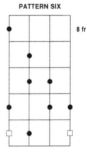
8 fr

PATTERN SEVEN
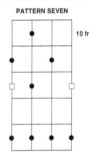
10 fr

(D–E–F–G–A–B–C♯)

PATTERN FOUR
5 fr

PATTERN FIVE
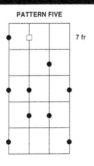
7 fr

PATTERN SIX
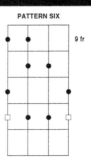
9 fr

PATTERN SEVEN
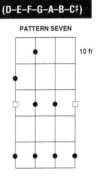
10 fr

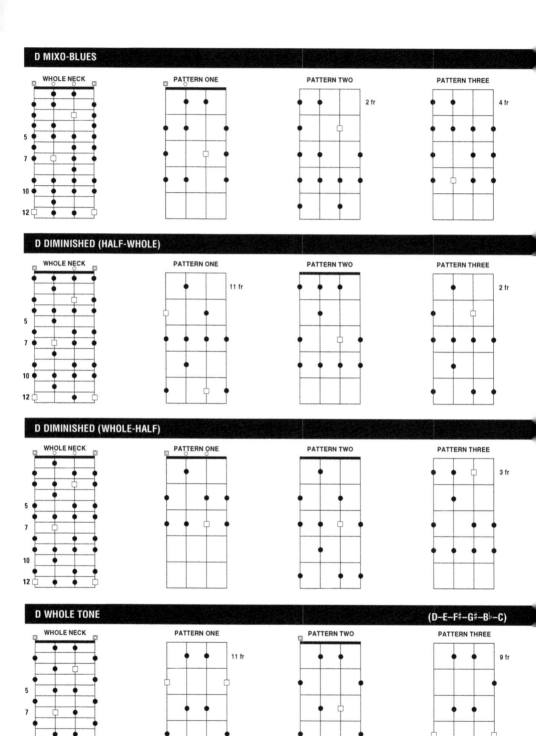

D

(D–E–F–F♯–G–G♯–A–B–C)

PATTERN FOUR
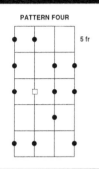
5 fr

PATTERN FIVE
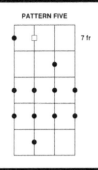
7 fr

PATTERN SIX
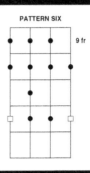
9 fr

PATTERN SEVEN
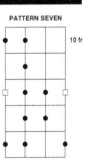
10 fr

(D–E♭–F–G♭–A♭–A–B–C)

PATTERN FOUR
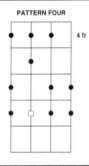
4 fr

PATTERN FIVE
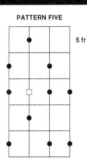
5 fr

PATTERN SIX
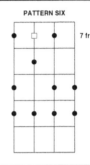
7 fr

PATTERN SEVEN
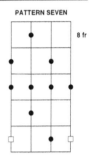
8 fr

(D–E–F–G–A♭–B♭–B–C♯)

PATTERN FOUR
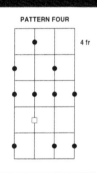
4 fr

PATTERN FIVE
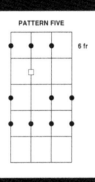
6 fr

PATTERN SIX
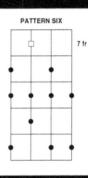
7 fr

PATTERN SEVEN
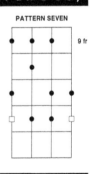
9 fr

D CHROMATIC (D–D♯–E–F–F♯–G–G♯–A–A♯–B–C–C♯)

WHOLE NECK
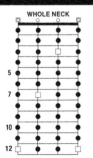

PATTERN ONE
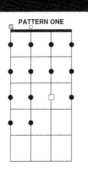

PATTERN TWO / THREE
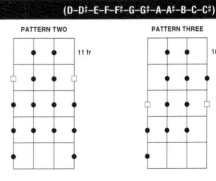
11 fr · 10 fr

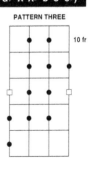

39

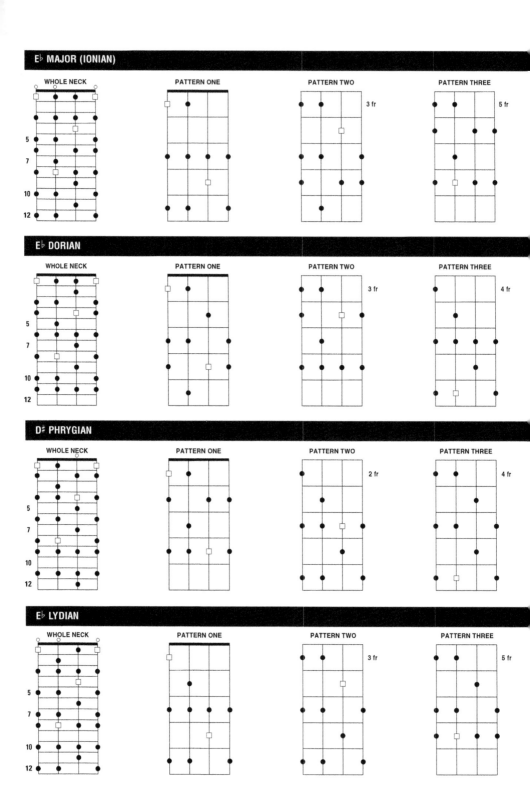

Eb MAJOR (IONIAN)

WHOLE NECK   PATTERN ONE   PATTERN TWO   PATTERN THREE

Eb DORIAN

WHOLE NECK   PATTERN ONE   PATTERN TWO   PATTERN THREE

D# PHRYGIAN

WHOLE NECK   PATTERN ONE   PATTERN TWO   PATTERN THREE

Eb LYDIAN

WHOLE NECK   PATTERN ONE   PATTERN TWO   PATTERN THREE

(E♭–F–G–A♭–B♭–C–D)

PATTERN FOUR
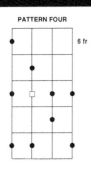
6 fr

PATTERN FIVE
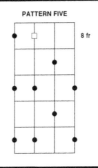
8 fr

PATTERN SIX
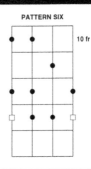
10 fr

PATTERN SEVEN
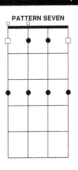

(E♭–F–G♭–A♭–B♭–C–D♭)

PATTERN FOUR
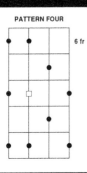
6 fr

PATTERN FIVE
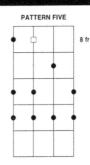
8 fr

PATTERN SIX
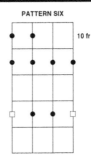
10 fr

PATTERN SEVEN
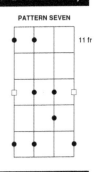
11 fr

(D#–E–F#–G#–A#–B–C#)

PATTERN FOUR
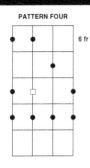
6 fr

PATTERN FIVE
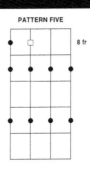
8 fr

PATTERN SIX
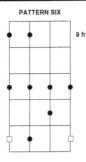
9 fr

PATTERN SEVEN
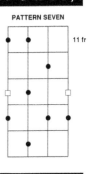
11 fr

(E♭–F–G–A–B♭–C–D)

PATTERN FOUR
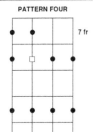
7 fr

PATTERN FIVE
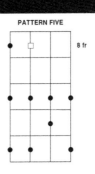
8 fr

PATTERN SIX
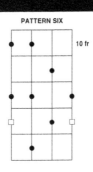
10 fr

PATTERN SEVEN
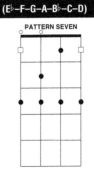

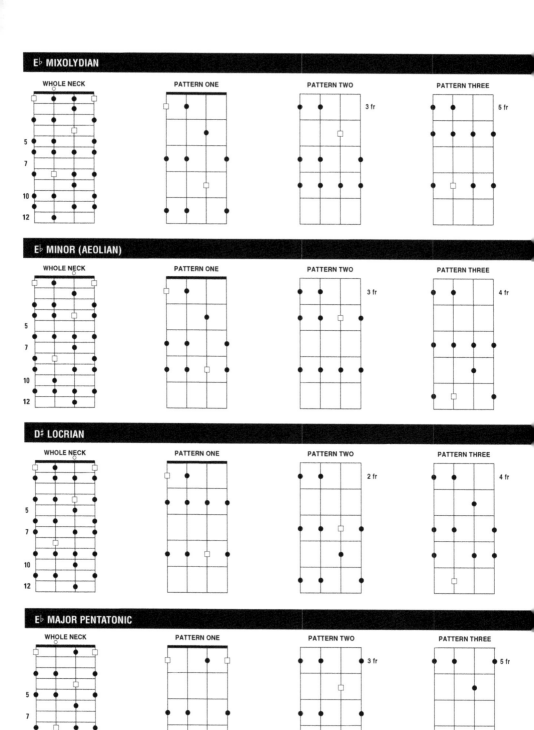

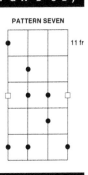

D#/E♭

(E♭–F–G–A♭–B♭–C–D♭)

PATTERN FOUR	PATTERN FIVE	PATTERN SIX	PATTERN SEVEN

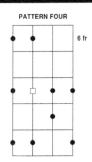 6 fr
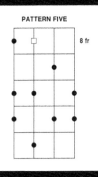 8 fr
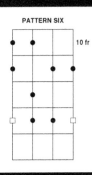 10 fr
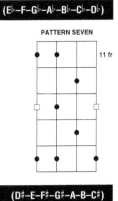 11 fr

(E♭–F–G♭–A♭–B♭–C♭–D♭)

PATTERN FOUR	PATTERN FIVE	PATTERN SIX	PATTERN SEVEN

6 fr
8 fr
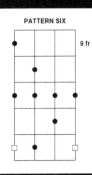 9 fr
11 fr

(D#–E–F#–G#–A–B–C#)

PATTERN FOUR	PATTERN FIVE	PATTERN SIX	PATTERN SEVEN

6 fr
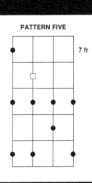 7 fr
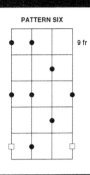 9 fr
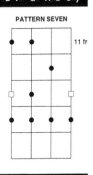 11 fr

(E♭–F–G–B♭–C)

PATTERN FOUR	PATTERN FIVE	ALT. PATTERN ONE	ALT. PATTERN TWO

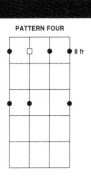 8 fr
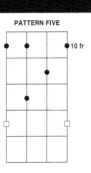 10 fr
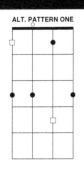
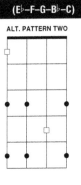

43

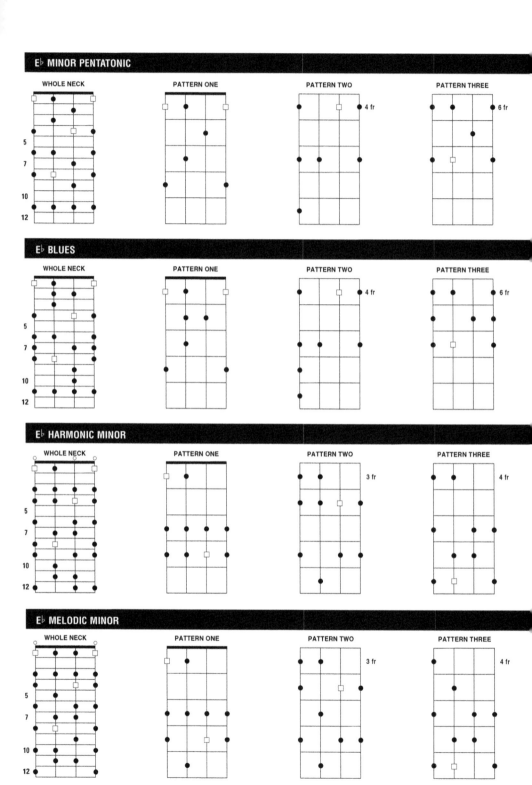

E♭ MINOR PENTATONIC

WHOLE NECK   PATTERN ONE   PATTERN TWO   PATTERN THREE

E♭ BLUES

WHOLE NECK   PATTERN ONE   PATTERN TWO   PATTERN THREE

E♭ HARMONIC MINOR

WHOLE NECK   PATTERN ONE   PATTERN TWO   PATTERN THREE

E♭ MELODIC MINOR

WHOLE NECK   PATTERN ONE   PATTERN TWO   PATTERN THREE

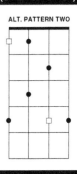

D♯/E♭

(E♭–G♭–A–B♭–D♭)

PATTERN FOUR	PATTERN FIVE	ALT. PATTERN ONE	ALT. PATTERN TWO

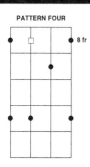 8 fr

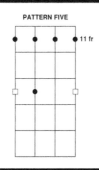 11 fr

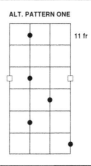 11 fr

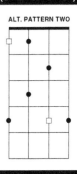

(E♭–G♭–A♭–A–B♭–D♭)

PATTERN FOUR	PATTERN FIVE	ALT. PATTERN ONE	ALT. PATTERN TWO

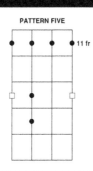 8 fr

11 fr

11 fr

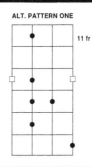

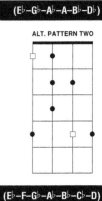

(E♭–F–G♭–A♭–B♭–C♭–D)

PATTERN FOUR	PATTERN FIVE	PATTERN SIX	PATTERN SEVEN

6 fr

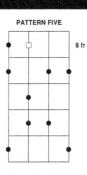 8 fr

9 fr

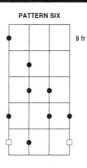 11 fr

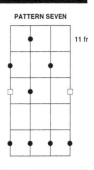

(E♭–F–G♭–A♭–B♭–C–D)

PATTERN FOUR	PATTERN FIVE	PATTERN SIX	PATTERN SEVEN

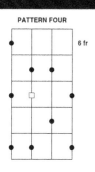 6 fr

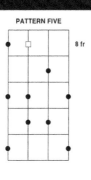 8 fr

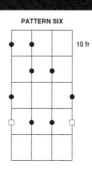 10 fr

11 fr

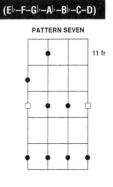

45

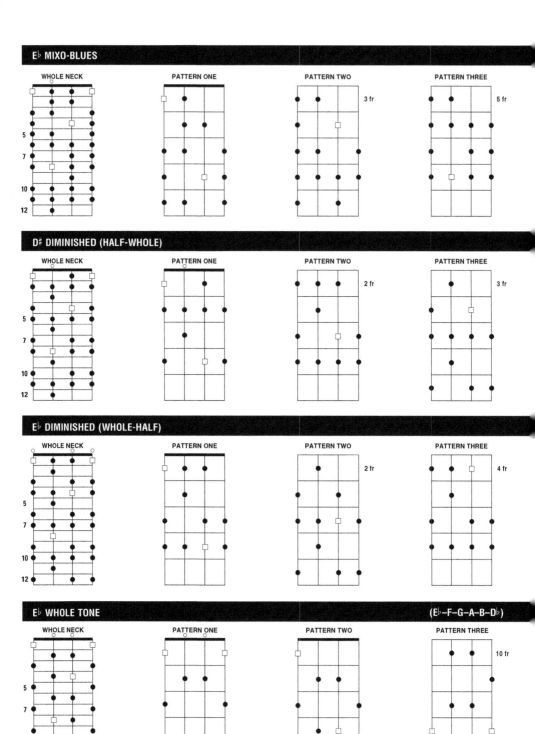

E♭ MIXO-BLUES

D# DIMINISHED (HALF-WHOLE)

E♭ DIMINISHED (WHOLE-HALF)

E♭ WHOLE TONE   (E♭–F–G–A–B–D♭)

(E♭–F–F#–G–A♭–A–B♭–C–D♭)

PATTERN FOUR	PATTERN FIVE	PATTERN SIX	PATTERN SEVEN
6 fr	8 fr	10 fr	11 fr

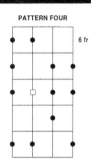
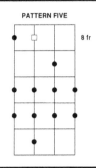
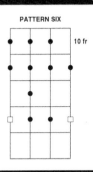
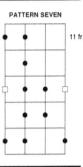

(D#–E–F#–G–A–B♭–C–C#)

PATTERN FOUR	PATTERN FIVE	PATTERN SIX	PATTERN SEVEN
5 fr	6 fr	8 fr	9 fr

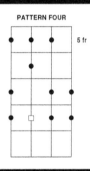
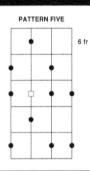
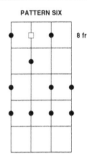
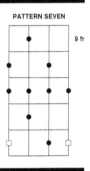

(E♭–F–G♭–A♭–A–B–C–D)

PATTERN FOUR	PATTERN FIVE	PATTERN SIX	PATTERN SEVEN
5 fr	7 fr	8 fr	10 fr

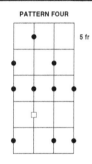
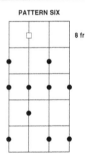
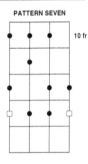

D# CHROMATIC   **(D#–E–F–F#–G–G#–A–A#–B–C–C#–D)**

WHOLE NECK	PATTERN ONE	PATTERN TWO	PATTERN THREE
			11 fr

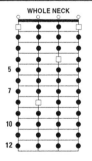
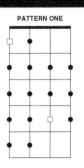
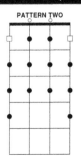
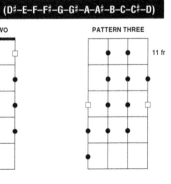

E MAJOR (IONIAN)

WHOLE NECK | PATTERN ONE | PATTERN TWO | PATTERN THREE

E DORIAN

WHOLE NECK | PATTERN ONE | PATTERN TWO | PATTERN THREE

E PHRYGIAN

WHOLE NECK | PATTERN ONE | PATTERN TWO | PATTERN THREE

E LYDIAN

WHOLE NECK | PATTERN ONE | PATTERN TWO | PATTERN THREE

48

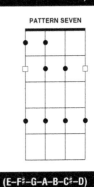

(E–F#–G#–A–B–C#–D#)

PATTERN FOUR   PATTERN FIVE   PATTERN SIX   PATTERN SEVEN

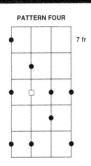 7 fr   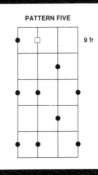 9 fr   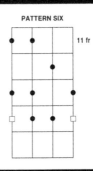 11 fr

(E–F#–G–A–B–C#–D)

PATTERN FOUR   PATTERN FIVE   PATTERN SIX   PATTERN SEVEN

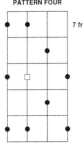 7 fr   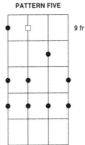 9 fr   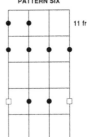 11 fr 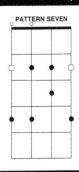

(E–F–G–A–B–C–D)

PATTERN FOUR   PATTERN FIVE   PATTERN SIX   PATTERN SEVEN

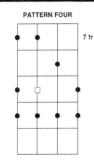 7 fr   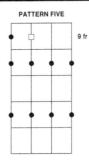 9 fr   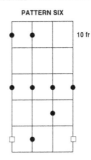 10 fr 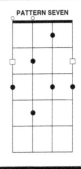

(E–F#–G#–A#–B–C#–D#)

PATTERN FOUR   PATTERN FIVE   PATTERN SIX   PATTERN SEVEN

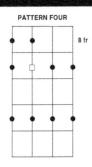 8 fr   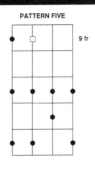 9 fr   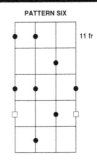 11 fr 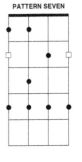

E MIXOLYDIAN

WHOLE NECK | PATTERN ONE | PATTERN TWO | PATTERN THREE

2 fr | 4 fr | 6 fr

E MINOR (AEOLIAN)

WHOLE NECK | PATTERN ONE | PATTERN TWO | PATTERN THREE

2 fr | 4 fr | 5 fr

E LOCRIAN

WHOLE NECK | PATTERN ONE | PATTERN TWO | PATTERN THREE

2 fr | 3 fr | 5 fr

E MAJOR PENTATONIC

WHOLE NECK | PATTERN ONE | PATTERN TWO | PATTERN THREE

2 fr | 4 fr | 6 fr

(E–F♯–G♯–A–B–C♯–D)

PATTERN FOUR	PATTERN FIVE	PATTERN SIX	PATTERN SEVEN

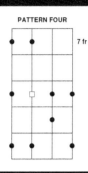 7 fr
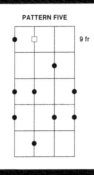 9 fr
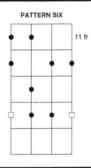 11 fr
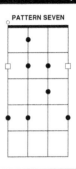

(E–F♯–G–A–B–C–D)

PATTERN FOUR	PATTERN FIVE	PATTERN SIX	PATTERN SEVEN

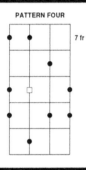 7 fr
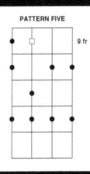 9 fr
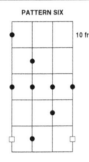 10 fr
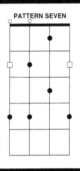

(E–F–G–A–B♭–C–D)

PATTERN FOUR	PATTERN FIVE	PATTERN SIX	PATTERN SEVEN

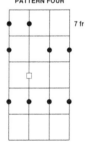 7 fr
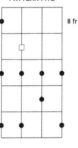 8 fr

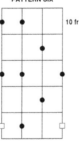 10 fr
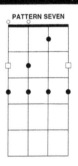

(E–F♯–G♯–B–C♯)

PATTERN FOUR	PATTERN FIVE	ALT. PATTERN ONE	ALT. PATTERN TWO

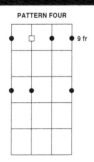 9 fr
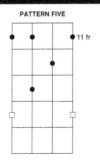 11 fr
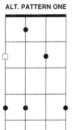
2 fr

51

E MINOR PENTATONIC

WHOLE NECK PATTERN ONE PATTERN TWO PATTERN THREE

E BLUES

WHOLE NECK PATTERN ONE PATTERN TWO PATTERN THREE

E HARMONIC MINOR

WHOLE NECK PATTERN ONE PATTERN TWO PATTERN THREE

E MELODIC MINOR

WHOLE NECK PATTERN ONE PATTERN TWO PATTERN THREE

(E–G–A–B–D)

PATTERN FOUR	PATTERN FIVE	ALT. PATTERN ONE	ALT. PATTERN TWO
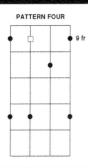 9 fr	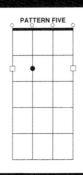	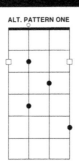	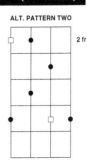 2 fr

(E–G–A–A♯–B–D)

PATTERN FOUR	PATTERN FIVE	ALT. PATTERN ONE	ALT. PATTERN TWO
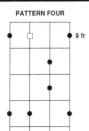 9 fr	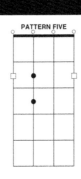	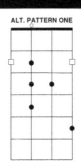	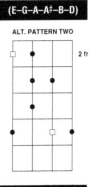 2 fr

(E–F♯–G–A–B–C–D♯)

PATTERN FOUR	PATTERN FIVE	PATTERN SIX	PATTERN SEVEN
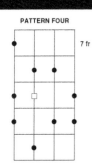 7 fr	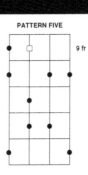 9 fr	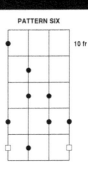 10 fr	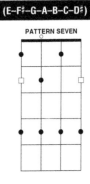

(E–F♯–G–A–B–C♯–D♯)

PATTERN FOUR	PATTERN FIVE	PATTERN SIX	PATTERN SEVEN
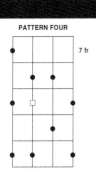 7 fr	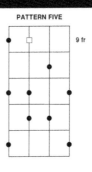 9 fr	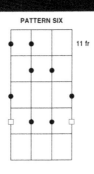 11 fr	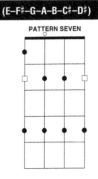

E MIXO-BLUES

WHOLE NECK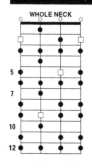

PATTERN ONE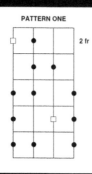
2 fr

PATTERN TWO
4 fr

PATTERN THREE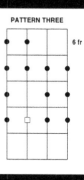
6 fr

E DIMINISHED (HALF-WHOLE)

WHOLE NECK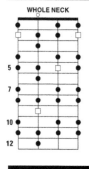

PATTERN ONE
PATTERN TWO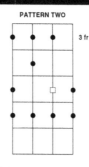
3 fr

PATTERN THREE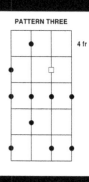
4 fr

E DIMINISHED (WHOLE-HALF)

WHOLE NECK

PATTERN ONE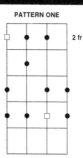
2 fr

PATTERN TWO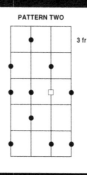
3 fr

PATTERN THREE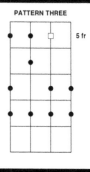
5 fr

E WHOLE TONE
(E–F#–G#–A#–C–D)

WHOLE NECK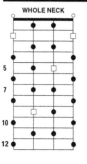

PATTERN ONE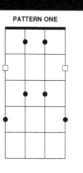

PATTERN TWO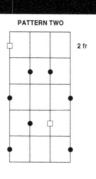
2 fr

PATTERN THREE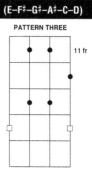
11 fr

(E–F♯–G–G♯–A–A♯–B–C♯–D)

PATTERN FOUR	PATTERN FIVE	PATTERN SIX	PATTERN SEVEN
7 fr	9 fr	11 fr	

(E–F–G–A♭–B♭–B–C♯–D)

PATTERN FOUR	PATTERN FIVE	PATTERN SIX	PATTERN SEVEN
6 fr	7 fr	9 fr	10 fr

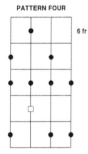
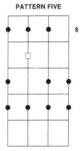
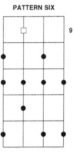
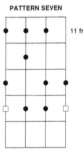

(E–F♯–G–A–B♭–C–C♯–D♯)

PATTERN FOUR	PATTERN FIVE	PATTERN SIX	PATTERN SEVEN
6 fr	8 fr	9 fr	11 fr

E CHROMATIC

(E–F–F♯–G–G♯–A–A♯–B–C–C♯–D–D♯)

WHOLE NECK	PATTERN ONE	PATTERN TWO	PATTERN THREE
	2 fr		

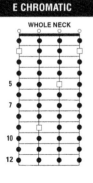
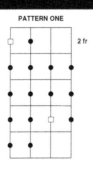
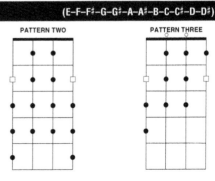

5
7
10
12

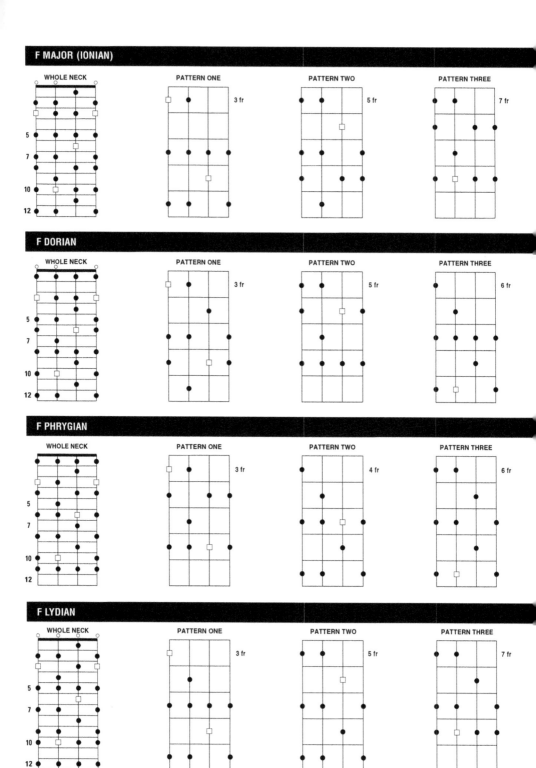

F MAJOR (IONIAN)

WHOLE NECK | PATTERN ONE (3 fr) | PATTERN TWO (5 fr) | PATTERN THREE (7 fr)

F DORIAN

WHOLE NECK | PATTERN ONE (3 fr) | PATTERN TWO (5 fr) | PATTERN THREE (6 fr)

F PHRYGIAN

WHOLE NECK | PATTERN ONE (3 fr) | PATTERN TWO (4 fr) | PATTERN THREE (6 fr)

F LYDIAN

WHOLE NECK | PATTERN ONE (3 fr) | PATTERN TWO (5 fr) | PATTERN THREE (7 fr)

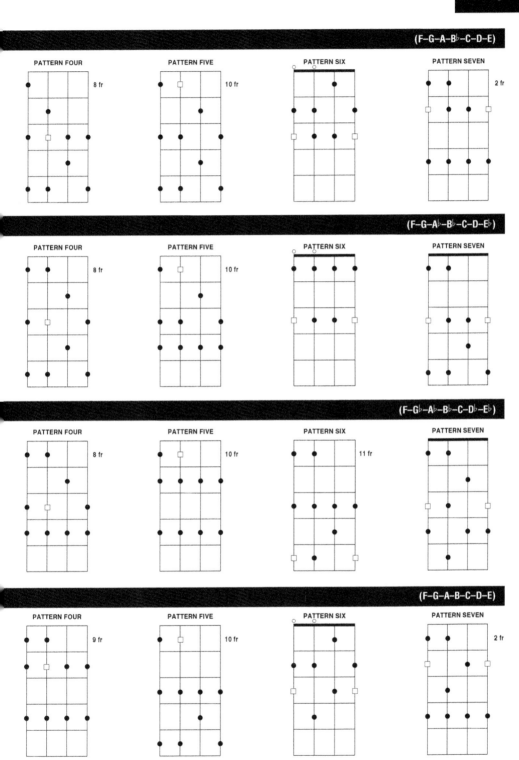

57

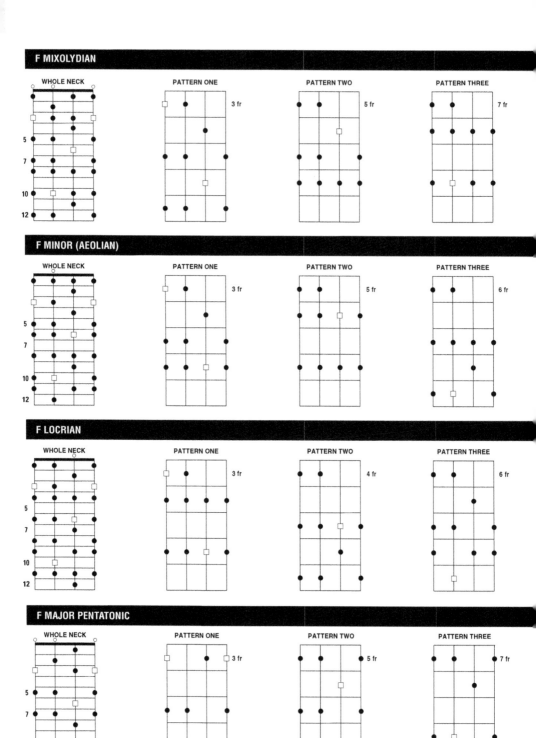

F MIXOLYDIAN

WHOLE NECK · PATTERN ONE 3 fr · PATTERN TWO 5 fr · PATTERN THREE 7 fr

F MINOR (AEOLIAN)

WHOLE NECK · PATTERN ONE 3 fr · PATTERN TWO 5 fr · PATTERN THREE 6 fr

F LOCRIAN

WHOLE NECK · PATTERN ONE 3 fr · PATTERN TWO 4 fr · PATTERN THREE 6 fr

F MAJOR PENTATONIC

WHOLE NECK · PATTERN ONE 3 fr · PATTERN TWO 5 fr · PATTERN THREE 7 fr

(F–G–A–B♭–C–D–E♭)

PATTERN FOUR
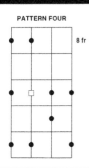
8 fr

PATTERN FIVE
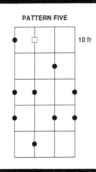
10 fr

PATTERN SIX
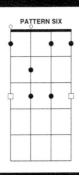

PATTERN SEVEN
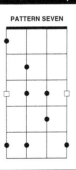

(F–G–A♭–B♭–C–D♭–E♭)

PATTERN FOUR
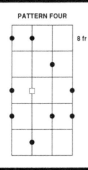
8 fr

PATTERN FIVE
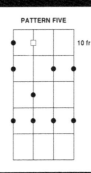
10 fr

PATTERN SIX
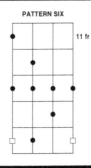
11 fr

PATTERN SEVEN
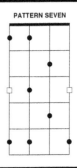

(F–G♭–A♭–B♭–C♭–D♭–E♭)

PATTERN FOUR
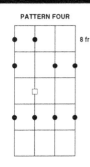
8 fr

PATTERN FIVE
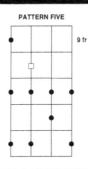
9 fr

PATTERN SIX
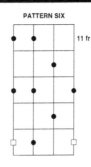
11 fr

PATTERN SEVEN
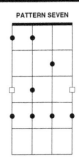

(F–G–A–C–D)

PATTERN FOUR
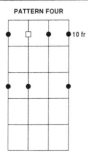
10 fr

PATTERN FIVE
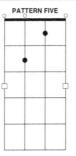

ALT. PATTERN ONE
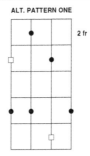
2 fr

ALT. PATTERN TWO
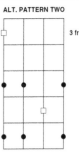
3 fr

F MINOR PENTATONIC

WHOLE NECK	PATTERN ONE	PATTERN TWO	PATTERN THREE
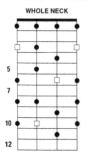	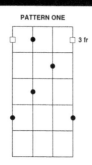	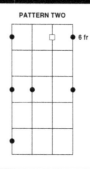	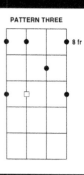

F BLUES

WHOLE NECK	PATTERN ONE	PATTERN TWO	PATTERN THREE
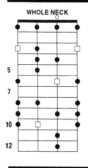	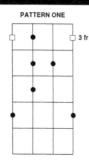	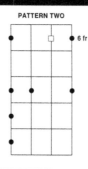	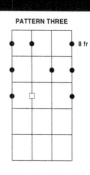

F HARMONIC MINOR

WHOLE NECK	PATTERN ONE	PATTERN TWO	PATTERN THREE
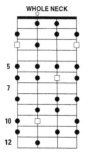	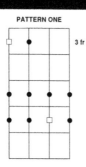	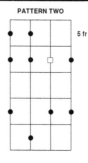	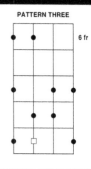

F MELODIC MINOR

WHOLE NECK	PATTERN ONE	PATTERN TWO	PATTERN THREE
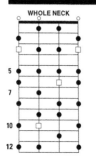	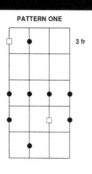	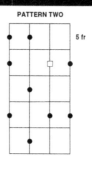	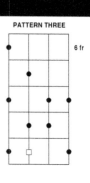

(F–A♭–B♭–C–E♭)

PATTERN FOUR   10 fr

PATTERN FIVE

ALT. PATTERN ONE

ALT. PATTERN TWO   3 fr

(F–A♭–B♭–B–C–E♭)

PATTERN FOUR   10 fr

PATTERN FIVE

ALT. PATTERN ONE

ALT. PATTERN TWO   3 fr

(F–G–A♭–B♭–C–D♭–E)

PATTERN FOUR   8 fr

PATTERN FIVE   10 fr

PATTERN SIX   11 fr

PATTERN SEVEN

(F–G–A♭–B♭–C–D–E)

PATTERN FOUR   8 fr

PATTERN FIVE   10 fr

PATTERN SIX

PATTERN SEVEN

61

F MIXO-BLUES

WHOLE NECK   PATTERN ONE (3 fr)   PATTERN TWO (5 fr)   PATTERN THREE (7 fr)

F DIMINISHED (HALF-WHOLE)

WHOLE NECK   PATTERN ONE (2 fr)   PATTERN TWO (4 fr)   PATTERN THREE (5 fr)

F DIMINISHED (WHOLE-HALF)

WHOLE NECK   PATTERN ONE (3 fr)   PATTERN TWO (4 fr)   PATTERN THREE (6 fr)

F WHOLE TONE   (F–G–A–B–C#–E♭)

WHOLE NECK   PATTERN ONE (2 fr)   PATTERN TWO (3 fr)   PATTERN THREE

(F–G–G♯–A–B♭–B–C–D–E♭)

PATTERN FOUR	PATTERN FIVE	PATTERN SIX	PATTERN SEVEN

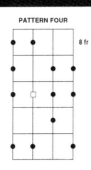 8 fr

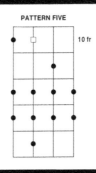 10 fr

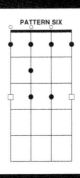

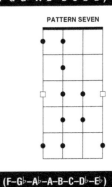

(F–G♭–A♭–A–B–C–D♭–E♭)

PATTERN FOUR	PATTERN FIVE	PATTERN SIX	PATTERN SEVEN

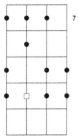 7 fr

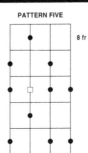 8 fr

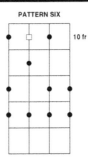 10 fr

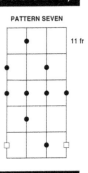 11 fr

(F–G–A♭–B♭–B–C♯–D–E)

PATTERN FOUR	PATTERN FIVE	PATTERN SIX	PATTERN SEVEN

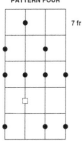 7 fr

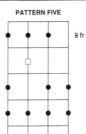 9 fr

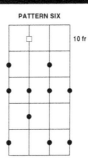 10 fr

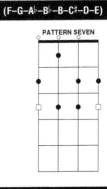

F CHROMATIC

(F–F♯–G–G♯–A–A♯–B–C–C♯–D–D♯–E)

WHOLE NECK	PATTERN ONE	PATTERN TWO	PATTERN THREE

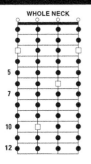

3 fr

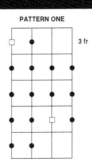 2 fr

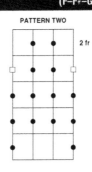

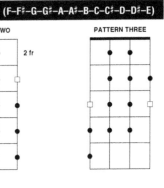

Gb MAJOR (IONIAN)

WHOLE NECK   PATTERN ONE   PATTERN TWO   PATTERN THREE

F# DORIAN

WHOLE NECK   PATTERN ONE   PATTERN TWO   PATTERN THREE

F# PHRYGIAN

WHOLE NECK   PATTERN ONE   PATTERN TWO   PATTERN THREE

Gb LYDIAN

WHOLE NECK   PATTERN ONE   PATTERN TWO   PATTERN THREE

(Gb–Ab–Bb–Cb–Db–Eb–F)

PATTERN FOUR	PATTERN FIVE	PATTERN SIX	PATTERN SEVEN

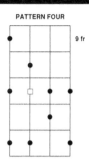 9 fr 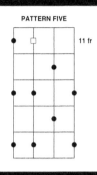 11 fr 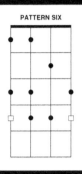 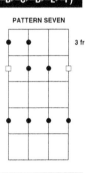 3 fr

(F#–G#–A–B–C#–D#–E)

PATTERN FOUR	PATTERN FIVE	PATTERN SIX	PATTERN SEVEN

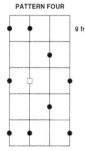 9 fr 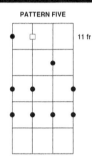 11 fr 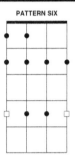 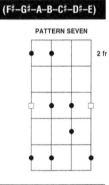 2 fr

(F#–G–A–B–C#–D–E)

PATTERN FOUR	PATTERN FIVE	PATTERN SIX	PATTERN SEVEN

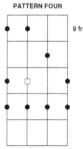 9 fr 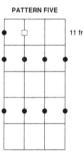 11 fr 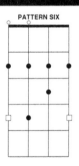 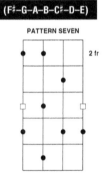 2 fr

(Gb–Ab–Bb–C–Db–Eb–F)

PATTERN FOUR	PATTERN FIVE	PATTERN SIX	PATTERN SEVEN

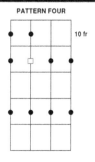 10 fr 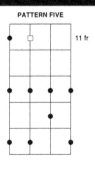 11 fr 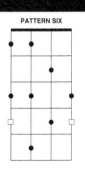 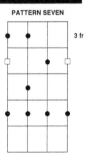 3 fr

F♯ MIXOLYDIAN

WHOLE NECK | PATTERN ONE | PATTERN TWO | PATTERN THREE

F♯ MINOR (AEOLIAN)

WHOLE NECK | PATTERN ONE | PATTERN TWO | PATTERN THREE

F♯ LOCRIAN

WHOLE NECK | PATTERN ONE | PATTERN TWO | PATTERN THREE

G♭ MAJOR PENTATONIC

WHOLE NECK | PATTERN ONE | PATTERN TWO | PATTERN THREE

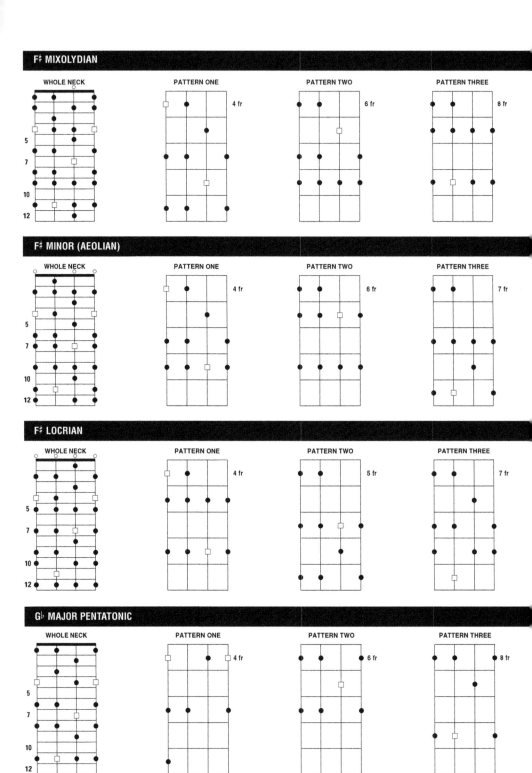

66

(F#–G#–A#–B–C#–D#–E)

PATTERN FOUR	PATTERN FIVE	PATTERN SIX	PATTERN SEVEN
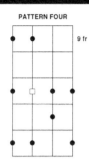 9 fr	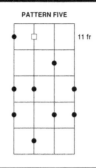 11 fr	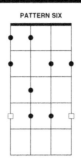	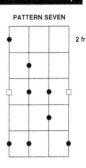 2 fr

(F#–G#–A–B–C#–D–E)

PATTERN FOUR	PATTERN FIVE	PATTERN SIX	PATTERN SEVEN
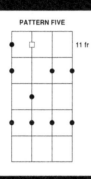 9 fr	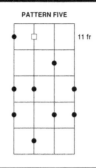 11 fr	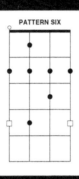	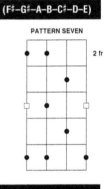 2 fr

(F#–G–A–B–C–D–E)

PATTERN FOUR	PATTERN FIVE	PATTERN SIX	PATTERN SEVEN
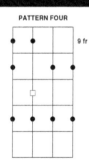 9 fr	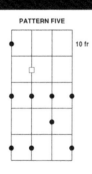 10 fr	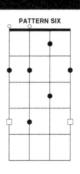	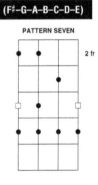 2 fr

(G♭–A♭–B♭–D♭–E♭)

PATTERN FOUR	PATTERN FIVE	ALT. PATTERN ONE	ALT. PATTERN TWO
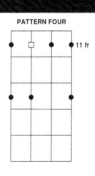 11 fr	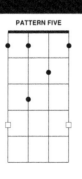	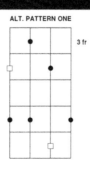 3 fr	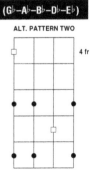 4 fr

F# MINOR PENTATONIC

WHOLE NECK	PATTERN ONE	PATTERN TWO	PATTERN THREE

F# BLUES

WHOLE NECK	PATTERN ONE	PATTERN TWO	PATTERN THREE

F# HARMONIC MINOR

WHOLE NECK	PATTERN ONE	PATTERN TWO	PATTERN THREE

F# MELODIC MINOR

WHOLE NECK	PATTERN ONE	PATTERN TWO	PATTERN THREE

68

F#/Gb

(F#–A–B–C#–E)

PATTERN FOUR
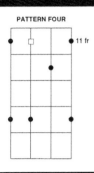
11 fr

PATTERN FIVE
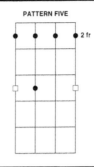
2 fr

ALT. PATTERN ONE
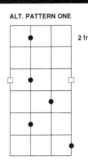
2 fr

ALT. PATTERN TWO
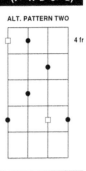
4 fr

(F#–A–B–C–C#–E)

PATTERN FOUR
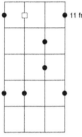
11 fr

PATTERN FIVE
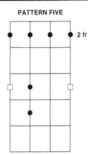
2 fr

ALT. PATTERN ONE
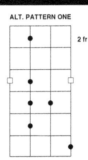
2 fr

ALT. PATTERN TWO
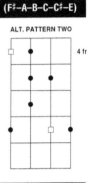
4 fr

(F#–G#–A–B–C#–D–E#)

PATTERN FOUR
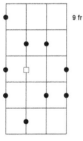
9 fr

PATTERN FIVE
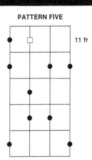
11 fr

PATTERN SIX
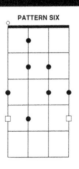

PATTERN SEVEN
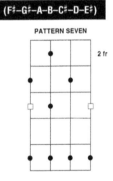
2 fr

(F#–G#–A–B–C#–D#–E#)

PATTERN FOUR
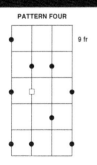
9 fr

PATTERN FIVE
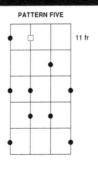
11 fr

PATTERN SIX
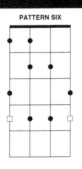

PATTERN SEVEN
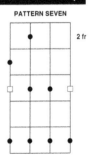
2 fr

69

F# MIXO-BLUES

WHOLE NECK | PATTERN ONE | PATTERN TWO | PATTERN THREE

F# DIMINISHED (HALF-WHOLE)

WHOLE NECK | PATTERN ONE | PATTERN TWO | PATTERN THREE

F# DIMINISHED (WHOLE-HALF)

WHOLE NECK | PATTERN ONE | PATTERN TWO | PATTERN THREE

G♭ WHOLE TONE   (G♭–A♭–B♭–C–D–E)

WHOLE NECK | PATTERN ONE | PATTERN TWO | PATTERN THREE

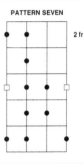

F#/Gb

(F#–G#–A–A#–B–C–C#–D#–E)

PATTERN FOUR	PATTERN FIVE	PATTERN SIX	PATTERN SEVEN

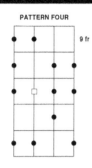 9 fr 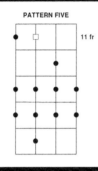 11 fr 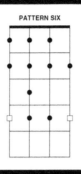 2 fr

(F#–G–A–Bb–C–Db–Eb–E)

PATTERN FOUR	PATTERN FIVE	PATTERN SIX	PATTERN SEVEN

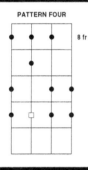 8 fr 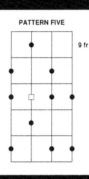 9 fr 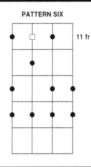 11 fr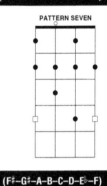

(F#–G#–A–B–C–D–Eb–F)

PATTERN FOUR	PATTERN FIVE	PATTERN SIX	PATTERN SEVEN

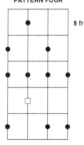 8 fr 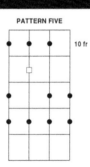 10 fr 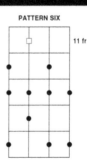 11 fr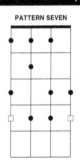

F# CHROMATIC (F#–G–G#–A–A#–B–C–C#–D–D#–E–E#)

WHOLE NECK	PATTERN ONE	PATTERN TWO	PATTERN THREE

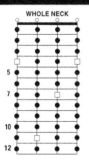 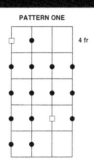 4 fr 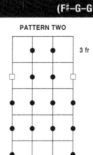 3 fr 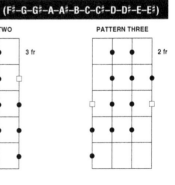 2 fr

71

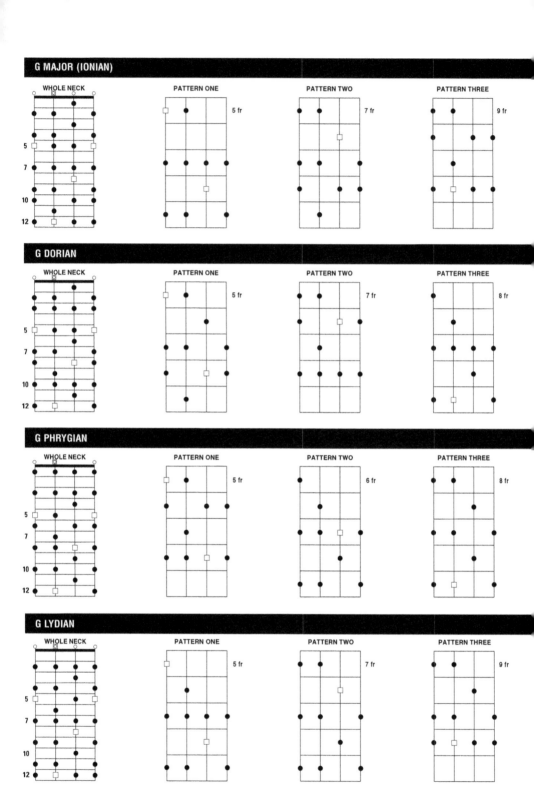

(G–A–B–C–D–E–F♯)

PATTERN FOUR	PATTERN FIVE	PATTERN SIX	PATTERN SEVEN
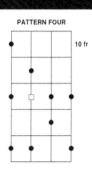 10 fr	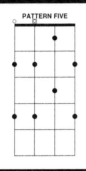	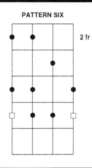 2 fr	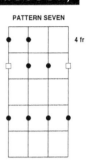 4 fr

(G–A–B♭–C–D–E–F)

PATTERN FOUR	PATTERN FIVE	PATTERN SIX	PATTERN SEVEN
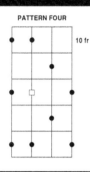 10 fr	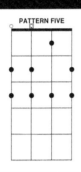	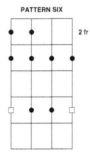 2 fr	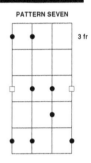 3 fr

(G–A♭–B♭–C–D–E♭–F)

PATTERN FOUR	PATTERN FIVE	PATTERN SIX	PATTERN SEVEN
10 fr		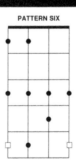	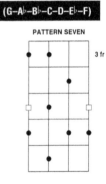 3 fr
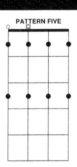			

(G–A–B–C♯–D–E–F♯)

PATTERN FOUR	PATTERN FIVE	PATTERN SIX	PATTERN SEVEN
11 fr	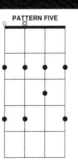	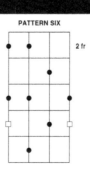 2 fr	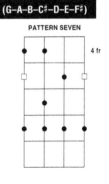 4 fr

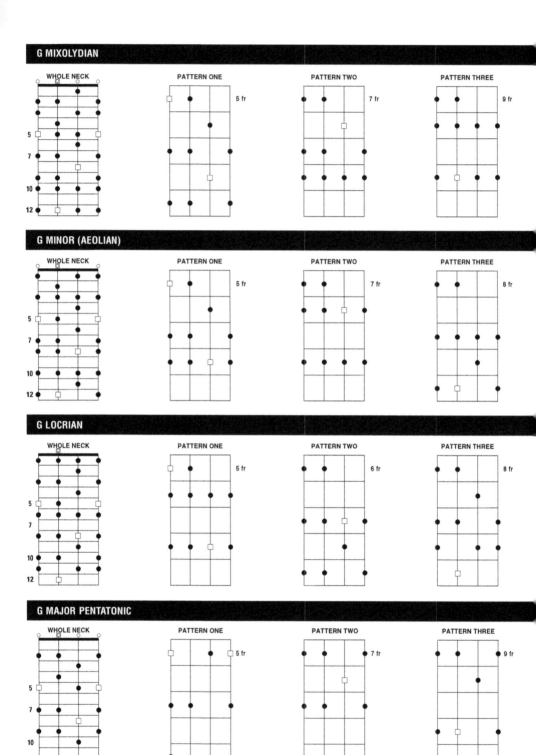

(G–A–B–C–D–E–F)

PATTERN FOUR	PATTERN FIVE	PATTERN SIX	PATTERN SEVEN
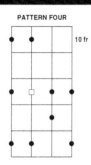 10 fr	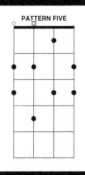	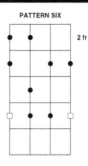 2 fr	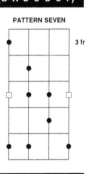 3 fr

(G–A–B♭–C–D–E♭–F)

PATTERN FOUR	PATTERN FIVE	PATTERN SIX	PATTERN SEVEN
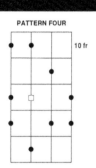 10 fr	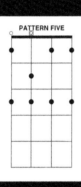	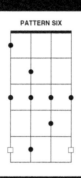	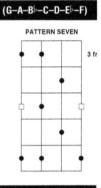 3 fr

(G–A♭–B♭–C–D♭–E♭–F)

PATTERN FOUR	PATTERN FIVE	PATTERN SIX	PATTERN SEVEN
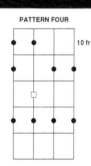 10 fr	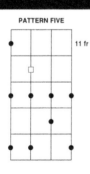 11 fr	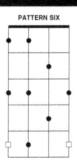	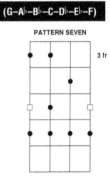 3 fr

(G–A–B–D–E)

PATTERN FOUR	PATTERN FIVE	ALT. PATTERN ONE	ALT. PATTERN TWO
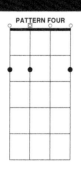	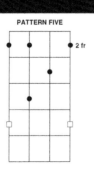 2 fr	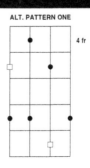 4 fr	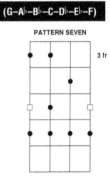 5 fr

75

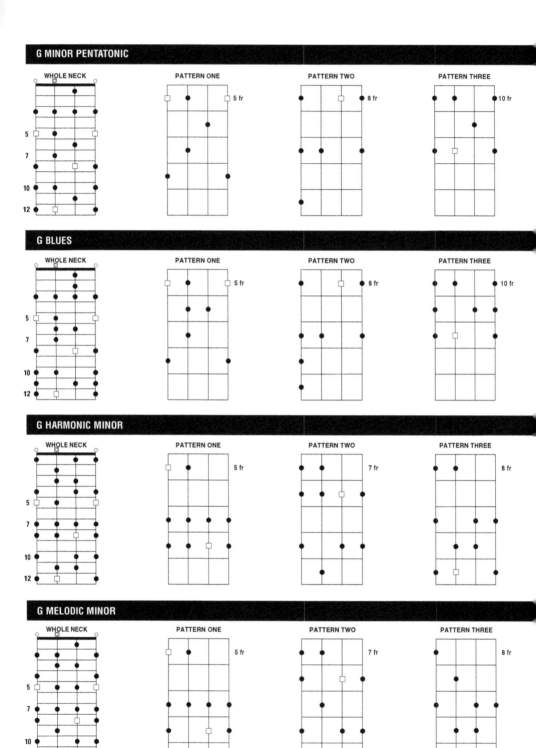

G MINOR PENTATONIC

WHOLE NECK | PATTERN ONE | PATTERN TWO | PATTERN THREE

G BLUES

WHOLE NECK | PATTERN ONE | PATTERN TWO | PATTERN THREE

G HARMONIC MINOR

WHOLE NECK | PATTERN ONE | PATTERN TWO | PATTERN THREE

G MELODIC MINOR

WHOLE NECK | PATTERN ONE | PATTERN TWO | PATTERN THREE

76

(G–B♭–C–D–F)

PATTERN FOUR

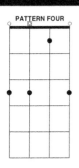

PATTERN FIVE

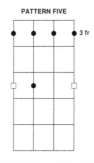
3 fr

ALT. PATTERN ONE

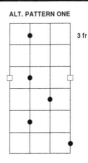
3 fr

ALT. PATTERN TWO

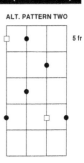
5 fr

(G–B♭–C–C♯–D–F)

PATTERN FOUR

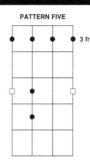

PATTERN FIVE

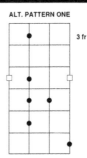
3 fr

ALT. PATTERN ONE

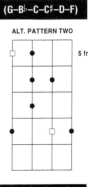
3 fr

ALT. PATTERN TWO

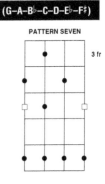
5 fr

(G–A–B♭–C–D–E♭–F♯)

PATTERN FOUR

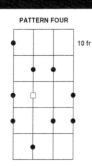
10 fr

PATTERN FIVE

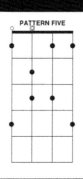

PATTERN SIX

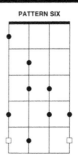

PATTERN SEVEN

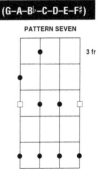
3 fr

(G–A–B♭–C–D–E–F♯)

PATTERN FOUR

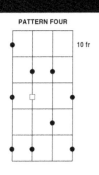
10 fr

PATTERN FIVE

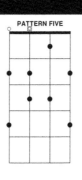

PATTERN SIX

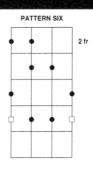
2 fr

PATTERN SEVEN
3 fr

G MIXO-BLUES

WHOLE NECK PATTERN ONE 5 fr PATTERN TWO 7 fr PATTERN THREE 9 fr

G DIMINISHED (HALF-WHOLE)

WHOLE NECK PATTERN ONE 4 fr PATTERN TWO 6 fr PATTERN THREE 7 fr

G DIMINISHED (WHOLE-HALF)

WHOLE NECK PATTERN ONE 5 fr PATTERN TWO 6 fr PATTERN THREE 8 fr

G WHOLE TONE (G–A–B–C#–E♭–F)

WHOLE NECK PATTERN ONE 4 fr PATTERN TWO 5 fr PATTERN THREE 2 fr

(G–A–A#–B–C–C#–D–E–F)

PATTERN FOUR 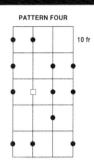 10 fr

PATTERN FIVE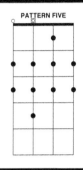

PATTERN SIX 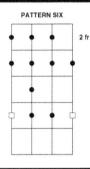 2 fr

PATTERN SEVEN 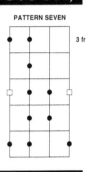 3 fr

(G–A♭–B♭–B–C#–D–E–F)

PATTERN FOUR 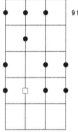 9 fr

PATTERN FIVE 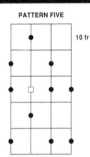 10 fr

PATTERN SIX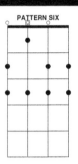

PATTERN SEVEN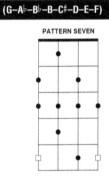

(G–A–B♭–C–D♭–E♭–E–F#)

PATTERN FOUR 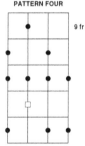 9 fr

PATTERN FIVE 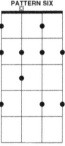 11 fr

PATTERN SIX

PATTERN SEVEN 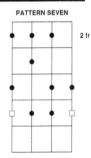 2 fr

G CHROMATIC **(G–G#–A–A#–B–C–C#–D–D#–E–F–F#)**

WHOLE NECK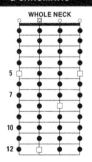

PATTERN ONE 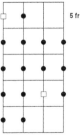 5 fr

PATTERN TWO 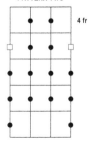 4 fr

PATTERN THREE 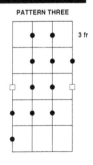 3 fr

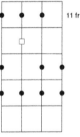

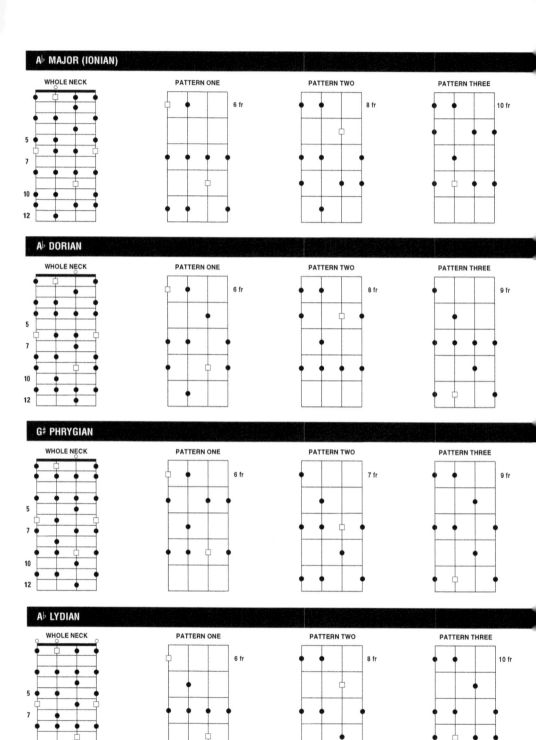

(A♭–B♭–C–D♭–E♭–F–G)

PATTERN FOUR	PATTERN FIVE	PATTERN SIX	PATTERN SEVEN
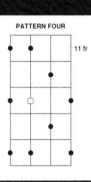 11 fr	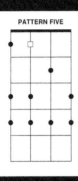	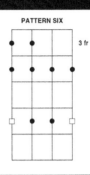 3 fr	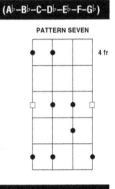 5 fr

(A♭–B♭–C–D♭–E♭–F–G♭)

PATTERN FOUR	PATTERN FIVE	PATTERN SIX	PATTERN SEVEN
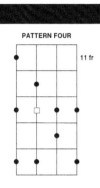 11 fr	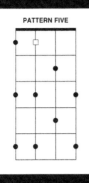	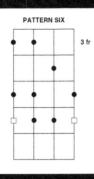 3 fr	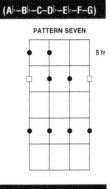 4 fr

(G#–A–B–C#–D#–E–F#)

PATTERN FOUR	PATTERN FIVE	PATTERN SIX	PATTERN SEVEN
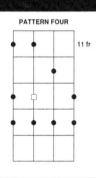 11 fr	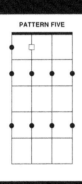	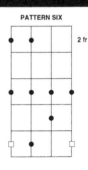 2 fr	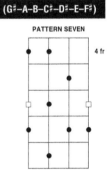 4 fr

(A♭–B♭–C–D–E♭–F–G)

PATTERN FOUR	PATTERN FIVE	PATTERN SIX	PATTERN SEVEN
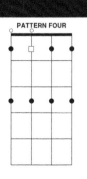	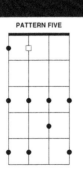	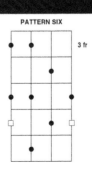 3 fr	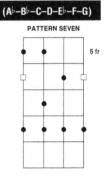 5 fr

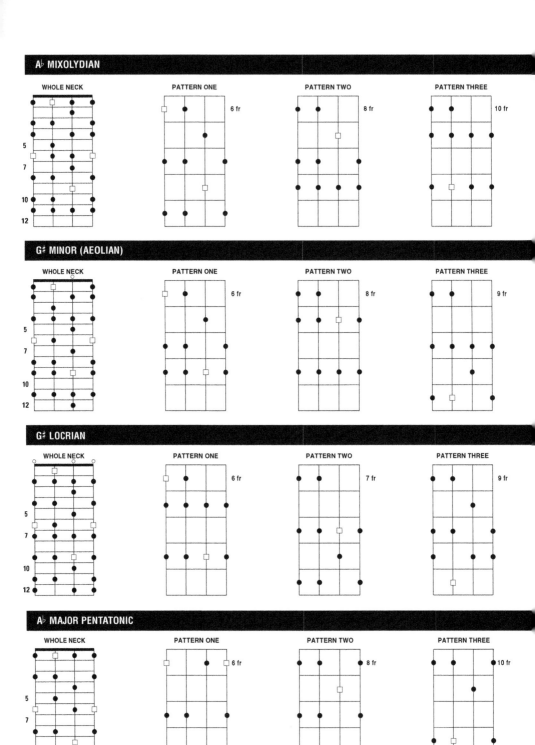

82

(Ab–Bb–C–Db–Eb–F–Gb)

PATTERN FOUR	PATTERN FIVE	PATTERN SIX	PATTERN SEVEN

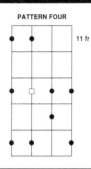 11 fr
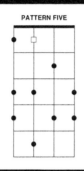
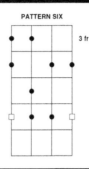 3 fr
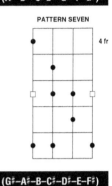 4 fr

(G#–A#–B–C#–D#–E–F#)

PATTERN FOUR	PATTERN FIVE	PATTERN SIX	PATTERN SEVEN

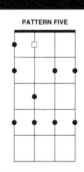 11 fr
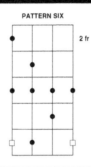 2 fr
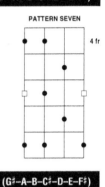 4 fr

(G#–A–B–C#–D–E–F#)

PATTERN FOUR	PATTERN FIVE	PATTERN SIX	PATTERN SEVEN

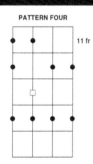 11 fr
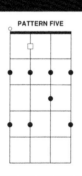
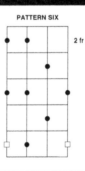 2 fr
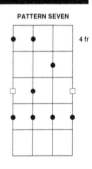 4 fr

(Ab–Bb–C–Eb–F)

PATTERN FOUR	PATTERN FIVE	ALT. PATTERN ONE	ALT. PATTERN TWO

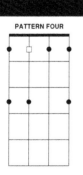
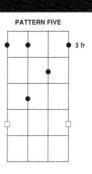 3 fr
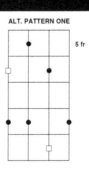 5 fr
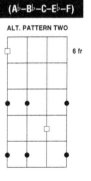 6 fr

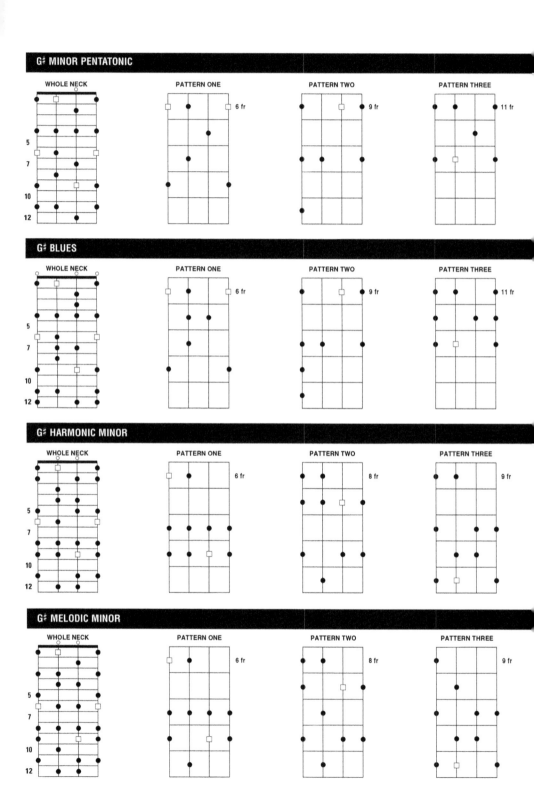

84

(G#–B–C#–D#–F#)

PATTERN FOUR	PATTERN FIVE	ALT. PATTERN ONE	ALT. PATTERN TWO

(G#–B–C#–D–D#–F#)

PATTERN FOUR	PATTERN FIVE	ALT. PATTERN ONE	ALT. PATTERN TWO

(G#–A#–B–C#–D#–E–F×)

PATTERN FOUR	PATTERN FIVE	PATTERN SIX	PATTERN SEVEN

(G#–A#–B–C#–D#–E#–F×)

PATTERN FOUR	PATTERN FIVE	PATTERN SIX	PATTERN SEVEN

85

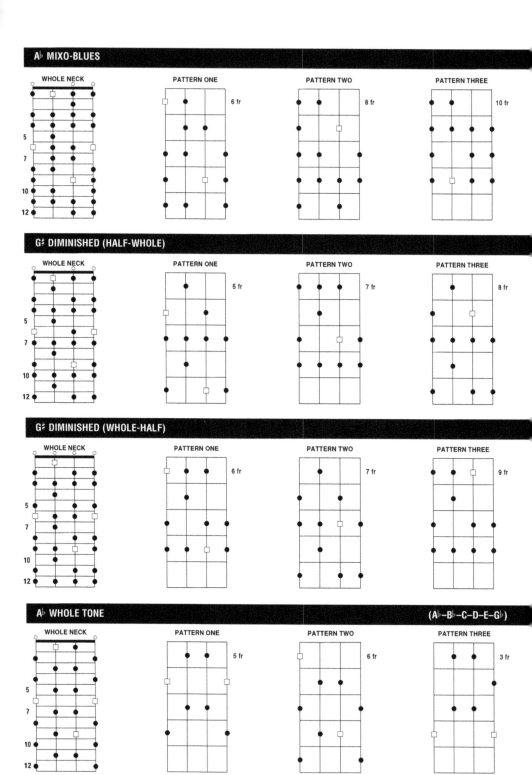

A♭ MIXO-BLUES

WHOLE NECK | PATTERN ONE — 6 fr | PATTERN TWO — 8 fr | PATTERN THREE — 10 fr

G♯ DIMINISHED (HALF-WHOLE)

WHOLE NECK | PATTERN ONE — 5 fr | PATTERN TWO — 7 fr | PATTERN THREE — 8 fr

G♯ DIMINISHED (WHOLE-HALF)

WHOLE NECK | PATTERN ONE — 6 fr | PATTERN TWO — 7 fr | PATTERN THREE — 9 fr

A♭ WHOLE TONE   (A♭–B♭–C–D–E–G♭)

WHOLE NECK | PATTERN ONE — 5 fr | PATTERN TWO — 6 fr | PATTERN THREE — 3 fr

(A♭–B♭–B–C–D♭–D–E♭–F–G♭)

PATTERN FOUR	PATTERN FIVE	PATTERN SIX	PATTERN SEVEN
11 fr		3 fr	4 fr

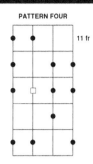
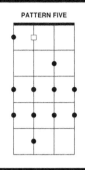
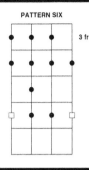
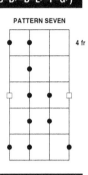

(G#–A–B–C–D–E♭–F–F#)

PATTERN FOUR	PATTERN FIVE	PATTERN SIX	PATTERN SEVEN
10 fr	11 fr		2 fr

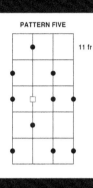
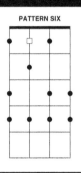
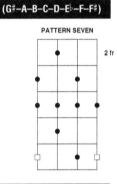

(G#–A#–B–C#–D–E–F–G)

PATTERN FOUR	PATTERN FIVE	PATTERN SIX	PATTERN SEVEN
10 fr			3 fr

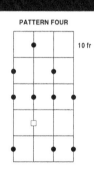
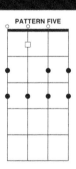
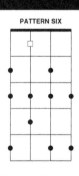
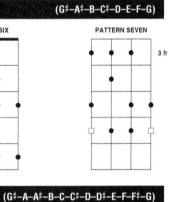

G# CHROMATIC   (G#–A–A#–B–C–C#–D–D#–E–F–F#–G)

WHOLE NECK	PATTERN ONE	PATTERN TWO	PATTERN THREE
	6 fr	5 fr	4 fr

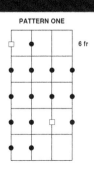
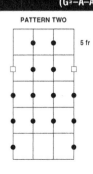

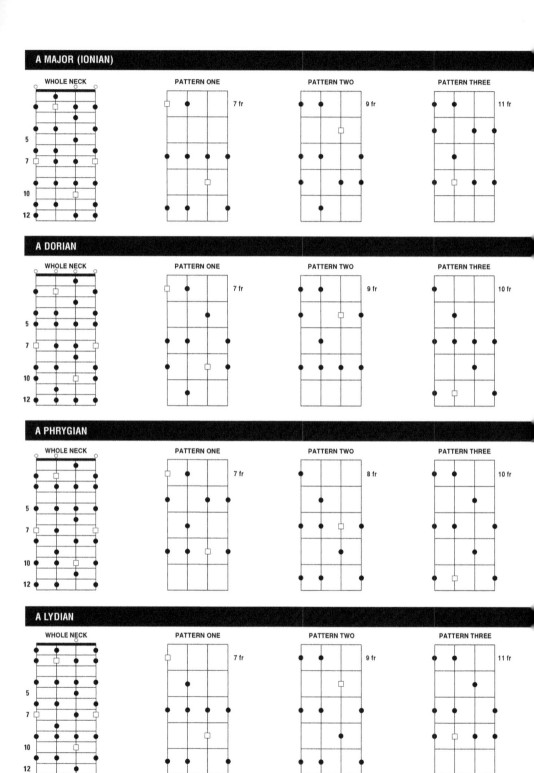

88

(A–B–C#–D–E–F#–G#)

PATTERN FOUR 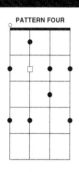 PATTERN FIVE 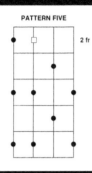 2 fr PATTERN SIX 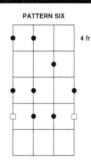 4 fr PATTERN SEVEN 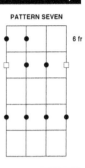 6 fr

(A–B–C–D–E–F#–G)

PATTERN FOUR 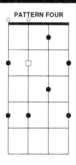 PATTERN FIVE 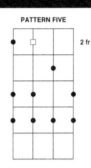 2 fr PATTERN SIX 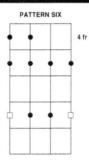 4 fr PATTERN SEVEN 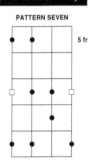 5 fr

(A–B♭–C–D–E–F–G)

PATTERN FOUR 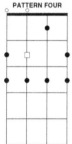 PATTERN FIVE 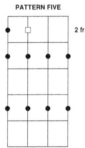 2 fr PATTERN SIX 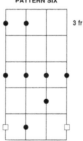 3 fr PATTERN SEVEN 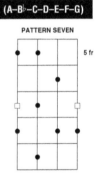 5 fr

(A–B–C#–D#–E–F#–G#)

PATTERN FOUR 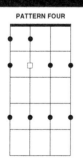 PATTERN FIVE 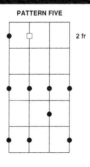 2 fr PATTERN SIX 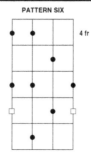 4 fr PATTERN SEVEN 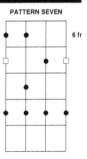 6 fr

A MIXOLYDIAN

WHOLE NECK	PATTERN ONE	PATTERN TWO	PATTERN THREE
	7 fr	9 fr	11 fr

A MINOR (AEOLIAN)

WHOLE NECK	PATTERN ONE	PATTERN TWO	PATTERN THREE
	7 fr	9 fr	10 fr

A LOCRIAN

WHOLE NECK	PATTERN ONE	PATTERN TWO	PATTERN THREE
	7 fr	8 fr	10 fr

A MAJOR PENTATONIC

WHOLE NECK	PATTERN ONE	PATTERN TWO	PATTERN THREE
	7 fr	9 fr	11 fr

(A–B–C#–D–E–F#–G)

PATTERN FOUR | PATTERN FIVE 2 fr | PATTERN SIX 4 fr | PATTERN SEVEN 5 fr

(A–B–C–D–E–F–G)

PATTERN FOUR | PATTERN FIVE 2 fr | PATTERN SIX 3 fr | PATTERN SEVEN 5 fr

(A–B♭–C–D–E♭–F–G)

PATTERN FOUR | PATTERN FIVE | PATTERN SIX 3 fr | PATTERN SEVEN 5 fr

(A–B–C#–E–F#)

PATTERN FOUR 2 fr | PATTERN FIVE 4 fr | ALT. PATTERN ONE 6 fr | ALT. PATTERN TWO 7 fr

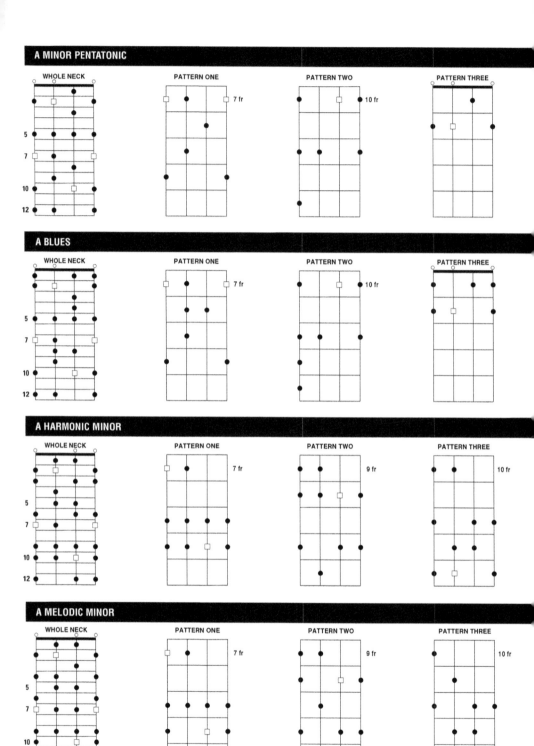

PATTERN FOUR PATTERN FIVE ALT. PATTERN ONE ALT. PATTERN TWO

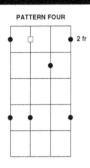 2 fr
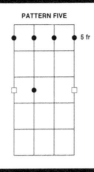 5 fr
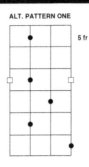 5 fr
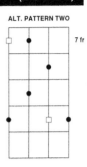 7 fr

PATTERN FOUR PATTERN FIVE ALT. PATTERN ONE ALT. PATTERN TWO

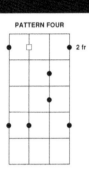 2 fr
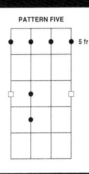 5 fr
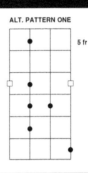 5 fr
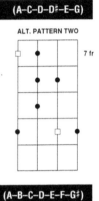 7 fr

PATTERN FOUR PATTERN FIVE PATTERN SIX PATTERN SEVEN

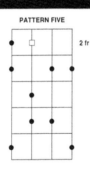
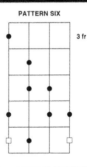 2 fr
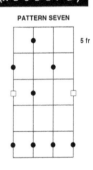 3 fr
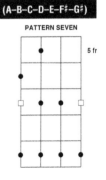 5 fr

PATTERN FOUR PATTERN FIVE PATTERN SIX PATTERN SEVEN

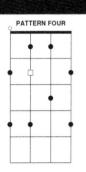
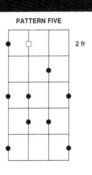 2 fr
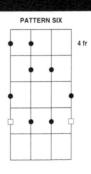 4 fr
5 fr

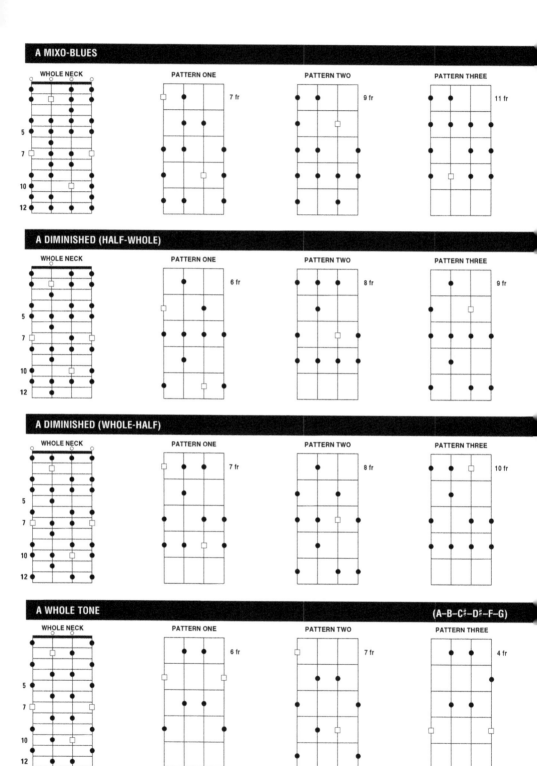

A MIXO-BLUES

WHOLE NECK | PATTERN ONE (7 fr) | PATTERN TWO (9 fr) | PATTERN THREE (11 fr)

A DIMINISHED (HALF-WHOLE)

WHOLE NECK | PATTERN ONE (6 fr) | PATTERN TWO (8 fr) | PATTERN THREE (9 fr)

A DIMINISHED (WHOLE-HALF)

WHOLE NECK | PATTERN ONE (7 fr) | PATTERN TWO (8 fr) | PATTERN THREE (10 fr)

A WHOLE TONE

(A–B–C#–D#–F–G)

WHOLE NECK | PATTERN ONE (6 fr) | PATTERN TWO (7 fr) | PATTERN THREE (4 fr)

(A–B–C–C♯–D–D♯–E–F♯–G)

PATTERN FOUR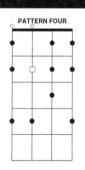

PATTERN FIVE 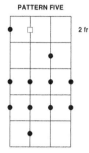 2 fr

PATTERN SIX 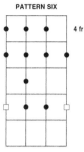 4 fr

PATTERN SEVEN 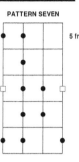 5 fr

(A–B♭–C–D♭–E♭–E–F♯–G)

PATTERN FOUR 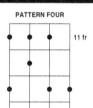 11 fr

PATTERN FIVE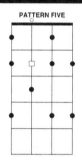

PATTERN SIX 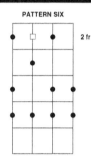 2 fr

PATTERN SEVEN 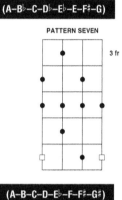 3 fr

(A–B–C–D–E♭–F–F♯–G♯)

PATTERN FOUR 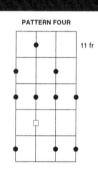 11 fr

PATTERN FIVE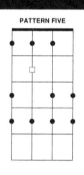

PATTERN SIX 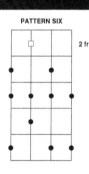 2 fr

PATTERN SEVEN 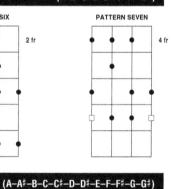 4 fr

A CHROMATIC   **(A–A♯–B–C–C♯–D–D♯–E–F–F♯–G–G♯)**

WHOLE NECK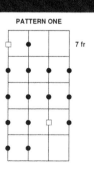

5
7
10
12

PATTERN ONE   7 fr

PATTERN TWO   6 fr

PATTERN THREE   5 fr

B♭ MAJOR (IONIAN)

WHOLE NECK · PATTERN ONE · PATTERN TWO · PATTERN THREE

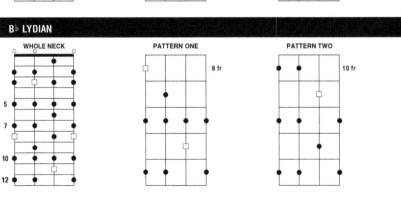

B♭ DORIAN

WHOLE NECK · PATTERN ONE · PATTERN TWO · PATTERN THREE

B♭ PHRYGIAN

WHOLE NECK · PATTERN ONE · PATTERN TWO · PATTERN THREE

B♭ LYDIAN

WHOLE NECK · PATTERN ONE · PATTERN TWO · PATTERN THREE

(Bb–C–D–Eb–F–G–A)

PATTERN FOUR	PATTERN FIVE	PATTERN SIX	PATTERN SEVEN
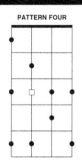	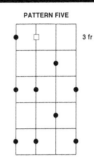 3 fr	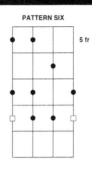 5 fr	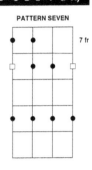 7 fr

(Bb–C–Db–Eb–F–G–Ab)

PATTERN FOUR	PATTERN FIVE	PATTERN SIX	PATTERN SEVEN
	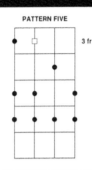 3 fr	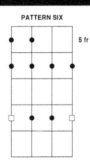 5 fr	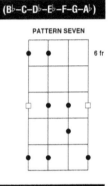 6 fr

(Bb–Cb–Db–Eb–F–Gb–Ab)

PATTERN FOUR	PATTERN FIVE	PATTERN SIX	PATTERN SEVEN
	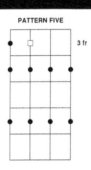 3 fr	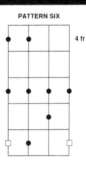 4 fr	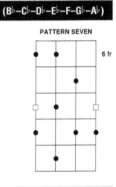 6 fr

(Bb–C–D–E–F–G–A)

PATTERN FOUR	PATTERN FIVE	PATTERN SIX	PATTERN SEVEN
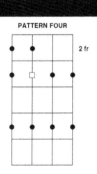 2 fr	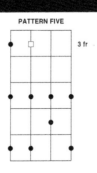 3 fr	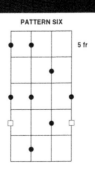 5 fr	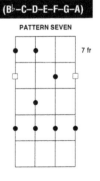 7 fr

Bb MIXOLYDIAN

WHOLE NECK | PATTERN ONE | PATTERN TWO | PATTERN THREE

Bb MINOR (AEOLIAN)

WHOLE NECK | PATTERN ONE | PATTERN TWO | PATTERN THREE

A# LOCRIAN

WHOLE NECK | PATTERN ONE | PATTERN TWO | PATTERN THREE

Bb MAJOR PENTATONIC

WHOLE NECK | PATTERN ONE | PATTERN TWO | PATTERN THREE

A#/B♭

(B♭–C–D–E♭–F–G–A♭)

PATTERN FOUR	PATTERN FIVE	PATTERN SIX	PATTERN SEVEN

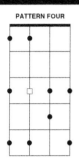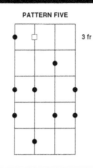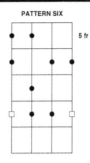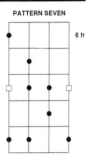

(B♭–C–D♭–E♭–F–G♭–A♭)

PATTERN FOUR	PATTERN FIVE	PATTERN SIX	PATTERN SEVEN

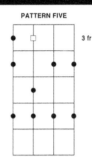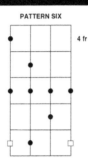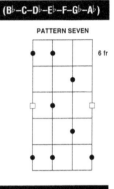

(A#–B–C#–D#–E–F#–G#)

PATTERN FOUR	PATTERN FIVE	PATTERN SIX	PATTERN SEVEN

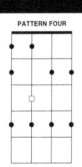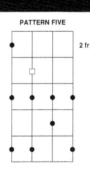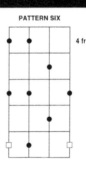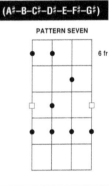

(B♭–C–D–F–G)

PATTERN FOUR	PATTERN FIVE	ALT. PATTERN ONE	ALT. PATTERN TWO

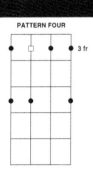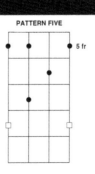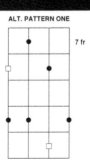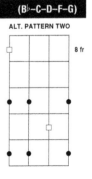

99

Bb MINOR PENTATONIC

| WHOLE NECK | PATTERN ONE | PATTERN TWO | PATTERN THREE |

Bb BLUES

| WHOLE NECK | PATTERN ONE | PATTERN TWO | PATTERN THREE |

Bb HARMONIC MINOR

| WHOLE NECK | PATTERN ONE | PATTERN TWO | PATTERN THREE |

Bb MELODIC MINOR

| WHOLE NECK | PATTERN ONE | PATTERN TWO | PATTERN THREE |

(B♭–D♭–E♭–F–A♭)

PATTERN FOUR	PATTERN FIVE	ALT. PATTERN ONE	ALT. PATTERN TWO

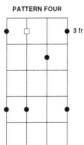
3 fr

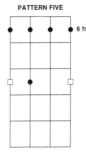
6 fr

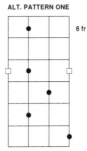
6 fr

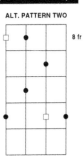
8 fr

(B♭–D♭–E♭–E–F–A♭)

PATTERN FOUR	PATTERN FIVE	ALT. PATTERN ONE	ALT. PATTERN TWO

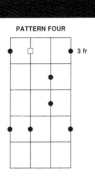
3 fr

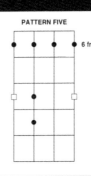
6 fr

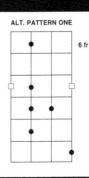
6 fr

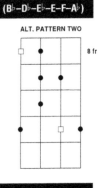
8 fr

(B♭–C–D♭–E♭–F–G♭–A)

PATTERN FOUR	PATTERN FIVE	PATTERN SIX	PATTERN SEVEN

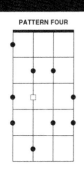

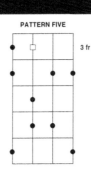
3 fr

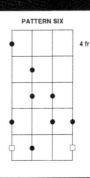
4 fr

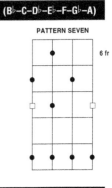
6 fr

(B♭–C–D♭–E♭–F–G–A)

PATTERN FOUR	PATTERN FIVE	PATTERN SIX	PATTERN SEVEN

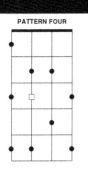

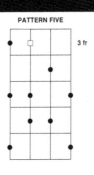
3 fr

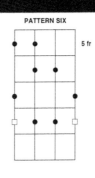
5 fr

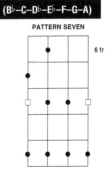
6 fr

101

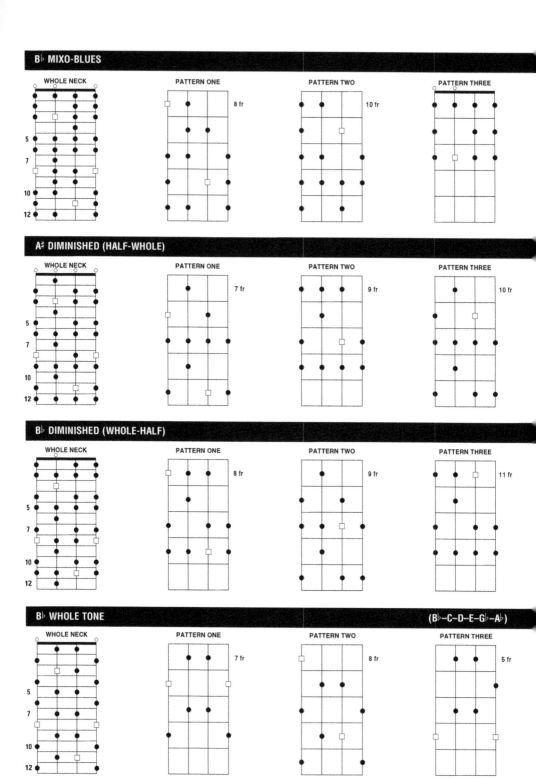

B♭ MIXO-BLUES

A♯ DIMINISHED (HALF-WHOLE)

B♭ DIMINISHED (WHOLE-HALF)

B♭ WHOLE TONE (B♭–C–D–E–G♭–A♭)

(Bb–C–C#–D–Eb–E–F–G–Ab)

PATTERN FOUR
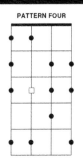

PATTERN FIVE
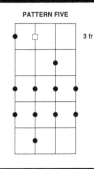
3 fr

PATTERN SIX
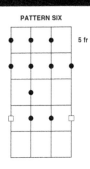
5 fr

PATTERN SEVEN
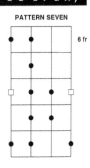
6 fr

(A#–B–C#–D–E–F–G–G#)

PATTERN FOUR
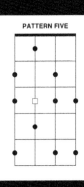

PATTERN FIVE
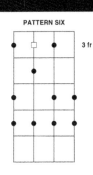

PATTERN SIX
3 fr

PATTERN SEVEN
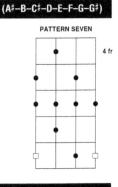
4 fr

(Bb–C–Db–Eb–E–F#–G–A)

PATTERN FOUR
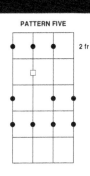

PATTERN FIVE
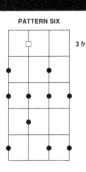
2 fr

PATTERN SIX
3 fr

PATTERN SEVEN
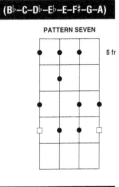
5 fr

Bb CHROMATIC

(Bb–B–C–C#–D–D#–E–F–F#–G–G#–A)

WHOLE NECK
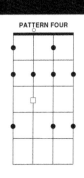
5
7
10
12

PATTERN ONE
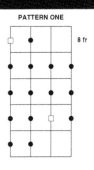
8 fr

PATTERN TWO
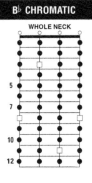
7 fr

PATTERN THREE
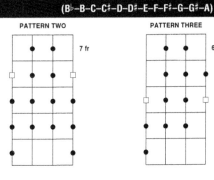
6 fr

103

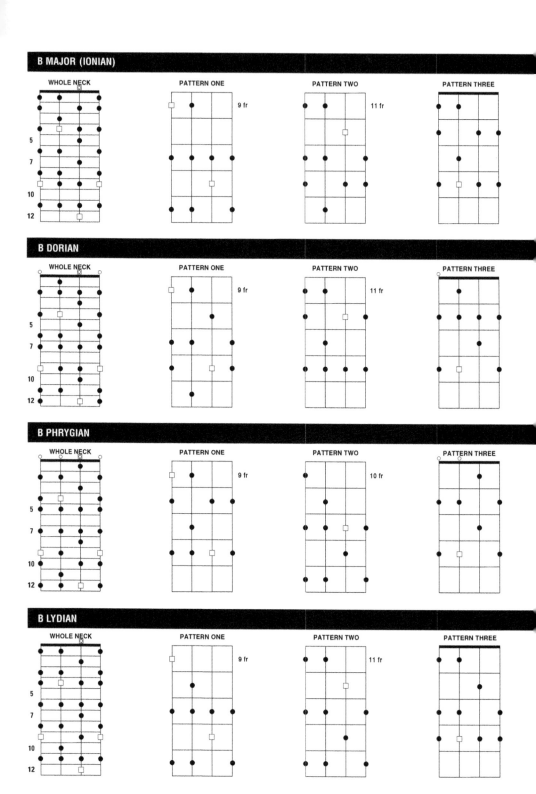

104

B

(B–C#–D#–E–F#–G#–A#)

PATTERN FOUR　　2 fr　　PATTERN FIVE　　4 fr　　PATTERN SIX　　6 fr　　PATTERN SEVEN　　8 fr

(B–C#–D–E–F#–G#–A)

PATTERN FOUR　　2 fr　　PATTERN FIVE　　4 fr　　PATTERN SIX　　6 fr　　PATTERN SEVEN　　7 fr

(B–C–D–E–F#–G–A)

PATTERN FOUR　　2 fr　　PATTERN FIVE　　4 fr　　PATTERN SIX　　5 fr　　PATTERN SEVEN　　7 fr

(B–C#–D#–E#–F#–G#–A#)

PATTERN FOUR　　3 fr　　PATTERN FIVE　　4 fr　　PATTERN SIX　　6 fr　　PATTERN SEVEN　　8 fr

B MIXOLYDIAN

WHOLE NECK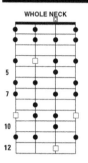

PATTERN ONE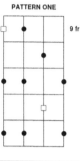
9 fr

PATTERN TWO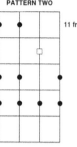
11 fr

PATTERN THREE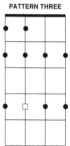

B MINOR (AEOLIAN)

WHOLE NECK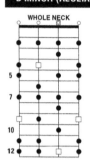

PATTERN ONE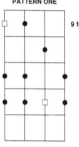
9 fr

PATTERN TWO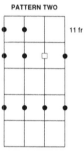
11 fr

PATTERN THREE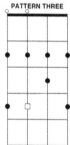

B LOCRIAN

WHOLE NECK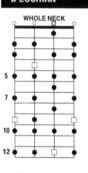

PATTERN ONE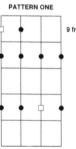
9 fr

PATTERN TWO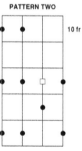
10 fr

PATTERN THREE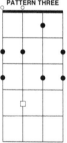

B MAJOR PENTATONIC

WHOLE NECK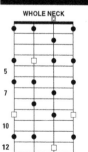

PATTERN ONE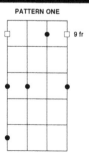
9 fr

PATTERN TWO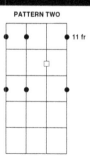
11 fr

PATTERN THREE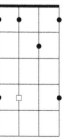

(B–C#–D#–E–F#–G#–A)

PATTERN FOUR
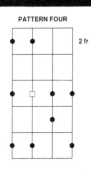
2 fr

PATTERN FIVE
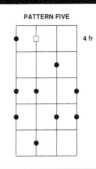
4 fr

PATTERN SIX
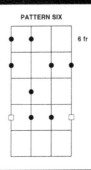
6 fr

PATTERN SEVEN
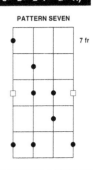
7 fr

(B–C#–D–E–F#–G–A)

PATTERN FOUR
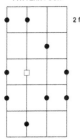
2 fr

PATTERN FIVE
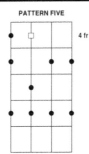
4 fr

PATTERN SIX
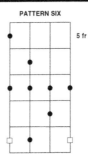
5 fr

PATTERN SEVEN
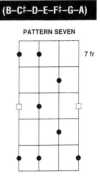
7 fr

(B–C–D–E–F–G–A)

PATTERN FOUR
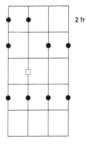
2 fr

PATTERN FIVE
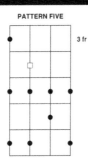
3 fr

PATTERN SIX
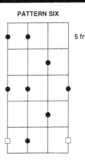
5 fr

PATTERN SEVEN
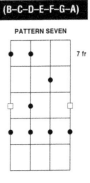
7 fr

(B–C#–D#–F#–G#)

PATTERN FOUR
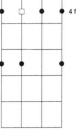
4 fr

PATTERN FIVE
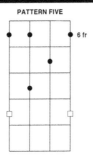
6 fr

ALT. PATTERN ONE
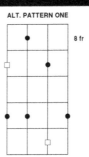
8 fr

ALT. PATTERN TWO
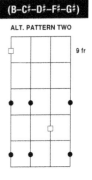
9 fr

B MINOR PENTATONIC

WHOLE NECK | PATTERN ONE | PATTERN TWO | PATTERN THREE

B BLUES

WHOLE NECK | PATTERN ONE | PATTERN TWO | PATTERN THREE

B HARMONIC MINOR

WHOLE NECK | PATTERN ONE | PATTERN TWO | PATTERN THREE

B MELODIC MINOR

WHOLE NECK | PATTERN ONE | PATTERN TWO | PATTERN THREE

(B–D–E–F♯–A)

PATTERN FOUR	PATTERN FIVE	ALT. PATTERN ONE	ALT. PATTERN TWO

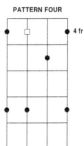 4 fr 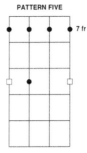 7 fr 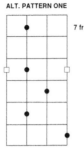 7 fr 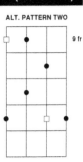 9 fr

(B–D–E–F–F♯–A)

PATTERN FOUR	PATTERN FIVE	ALT. PATTERN ONE	ALT. PATTERN TWO

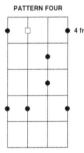 4 fr 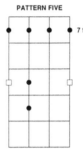 7 fr 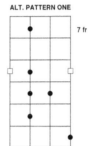 7 fr 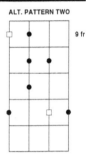 9 fr

(B–C♯–D–E–F♯–G–A♯)

PATTERN FOUR	PATTERN FIVE	PATTERN SIX	PATTERN SEVEN

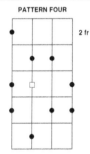 2 fr 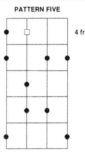 4 fr 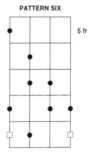 5 fr 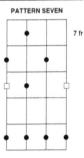 7 fr

(B–C♯–D–E–F♯–G♯–A♯)

PATTERN FOUR	PATTERN FIVE	PATTERN SIX	PATTERN SEVEN

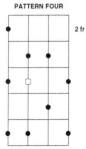 2 fr 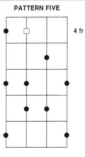 4 fr 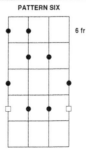 6 fr 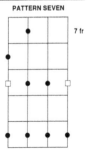 7 fr

B MIXO-BLUES

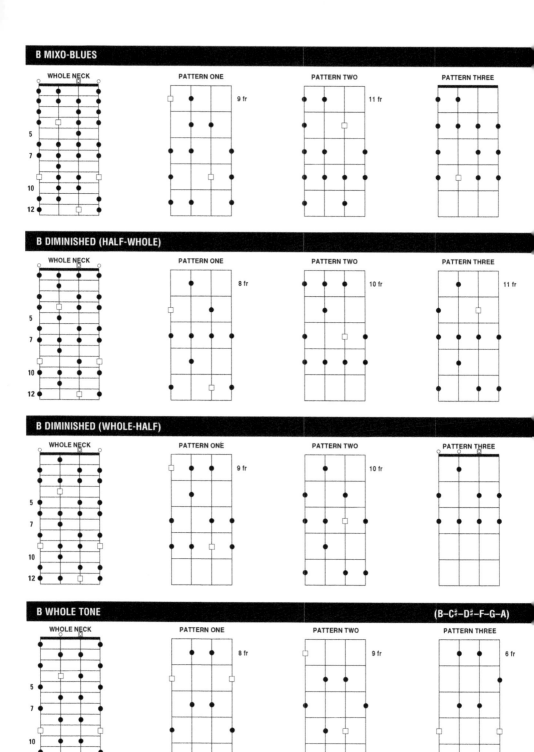

B DIMINISHED (HALF-WHOLE)

B DIMINISHED (WHOLE-HALF)

B WHOLE TONE

(B–C♯–D♯–F–G–A)

(B–C♯–D–D♯–E–F–F♯–G♯–A)

PATTERN FOUR   PATTERN FIVE   PATTERN SIX   PATTERN SEVEN

2 fr   4 fr   6 fr   7 fr

(B–C–D–E♭–F–G♭–A♭–A)

PATTERN FOUR   PATTERN FIVE   PATTERN SIX   PATTERN SEVEN

2 fr   4 fr   5 fr

(B–C♯–D–E–F–G–G♯–A♯)

PATTERN FOUR   PATTERN FIVE   PATTERN SIX   PATTERN SEVEN

3 fr   4 fr   6 fr

B CHROMATIC   **(B–C–C♯–D–D♯–E–F–F♯–G–G♯–A–A♯)**

WHOLE NECK   PATTERN ONE   PATTERN TWO   PATTERN THREE

5
7
10
12

9 fr   8 fr   7 fr

111

Learn To Play Today
with folk music instruction from

HAL•LEONARD®

Hal Leonard Banjo Method

This innovative method teaches 5-string, bluegrass style. The method consists of two instruction books and two cross-referenced supplement books that offer the beginner a carefully-paced and interest-keeping approach to the bluegrass style.

Method Book 1
00699500 Book...$6.95
00695101 Book/CD Pack...$16.95
Method Book 2
00699502 Book...$6.95
Supplementary Songbooks
00699515 Easy Banjo Solos..$6.95
00699516 More Easy Banjo Solos..$6.95

Hal Leonard Dulcimer Method
by Neal Hellman

A beginning method for the Appalachian dulcimer with a unique new approach to solo melody and chord playing. Includes tuning, modes and many beautiful folk songs all demonstrated on the audio accompaniment. Music and tablature.
00699289 Book...$6.95
00697230 Book/CD Pack..$14.95

Teach Yourself to Play the Folk Harp
by Sylvia Woods

This is the first book written exclusively for the folk harp that teaches the student how to play the instrument, step by step. Each of the 12 lessons includes instructions, exercises and folk and classical pieces using the new skills and techniques taught in the lesson.
00722251 Book...$12.95
00722252 Cassette...$7.95
00722253 Video...$54.95

The Hal Leonard Mandolin Method

This excellent mandolin method features play-along audio duets, great playable tunes in several styles (bluegrass, country, folk, blues), and standard music notation and tablature.
00699296 Book...$6.95
00695102 Book/CD Pack..$14.95

Jumpin' Jim's Ukulele Tips 'N' Tunes
A Beginner's Method and Songbook

Includes: Amazing Grace • Aura Lee • (Oh, My Darling) Clementine • Home on the Range • I've Been Working on the Railroad • My Country, 'Tis of Thee (America) • Oh! Susanna • The Star Spangled Banner • Swing Low, Sweet Chariot • When the Saints Go Marching In • and more.
00699406 Ukulele Technique...$12.95

FOR MORE INFORMATION, SEE YOUR LOCAL MUSIC DEALER,
OR WRITE TO:

HAL•LEONARD®
CORPORATION
7777 W. BLUEMOUND RD. P.O. BOX 13819 MILWAUKEE, WI 53213

Visit Hal Leonard Online at **www.halleonard.com**